Praise for *Performance Management*:

"Dr. Pulakos is one of the foremost experts on the practical application of performance management approaches. Based on her extensive expertise in this area she presents a down-to-earth, pragmatic approach that focuses on what you need to do to gain the best value from performance management and make your process work effectively. This book is useful for everyone involved in performance management – executives, managers, and human resources professionals."

Dr. Nancy Rotchford, Director, Associate Assessment Worldwide,
Ingram Micro, Inc.

"Elaine Pulakos provides an extremely insightful and useful book, the best ever written, to guide organizations in the design or redesign of their performance management systems. It emphasizes both strategic and tactical issues, with innumerable tips, best practices, and examples as guides to action."

Herbert G. Heneman III, Dickson-Bascom Professor Emeritus in Business,
University of Wisconsin-Madison

"Practical, user friendly, and highly engaging, this book reflects the author's considerable experience in designing, and, just as importantly, implementing performance management systems that yield tangible results."

Wayne F. Cascio, US Bank Term Professor of Management,
The Business School, University of Colorado Denver

"Anyone interested in designing and implementing a performance management system will be well served if they begin by consulting a new book entitled *Performance Management: A New Approach for Driving Business Results* by Elaine Pulakos. Pulakos provides the best information we have concerning research on performance management systems, and combines it with a list of 'best practices' to guide every step along the way. But what really sets this book part is that Pulakos then adds another layer and discusses the practical issues that may serve to limit exactly what a company can do in this area. She then goes even one step further and includes a series of training exercises to help guide the manager on how to develop and implement systems for performance management – not just performance appraisal – but the art of using appraisal information to help improve individual and organizational performance. This book is clearly written, practically oriented and yet based on scientific research. Stated simply, this is one of the finest examples of adapting scientific research for practice that I have seen anywhere."

Angelo S. DeNisi, Dean, A.B. Freeman School of Business,
Tulane University

Talent Management Essentials

Series Editor: Steven G. Rogelberg, Ph.D
Professor and Director Organizational Science, University of North Carolina – Charlotte

Senior Advisory Board:
- Eric Elder, Ph.D., Director, Talent Management, Corning Incorporated
- Bill Macey, Ph.D., Chief Executive Officer, Valtera Corporation
- Cindy McCauley, Ph.D., Senior Fellow, Center for Creative Leadership
- Elaine Pulakos, Ph.D., Chief Operating Officer, Personnel Decisions Research Institutes
- Doug Reynolds, Ph.D., Vice President, Assessment Technology, Development Dimensions International
- Ann-Marie Ryan, Ph.D., Professor, Michigan State University
- Lise Saari, Ph.D., Direct, Global Workforce Research, IBM
- John Scott, Ph.D., Vice President, Applied Psychological Techniques, Inc.
- Dean Stamoulis, Ph.D., Managing Director, Executive Assessment Practice Leader
- for the Americas, Russell Reynolds Associates

Special Features

Each volume contains a host of actual case studies, sample materials, tips, and cautionary notes. Issues pertaining to globalization, technology, and key executive points are highlighted throughout.

Titles in the Talent Management Essentials series:

Performance Management: A New Approach for Driving Business Results
Elaine D. Pulakos

Designing and Implementing Global Selection Systems
Ann-Marie Ryan and Nancy Tippins

Designing Workplace Mentoring Programs: An Evidence-based Approach
Tammy D. Allen, Lisa M. Finkelstein, and Mark L. Poteet

Career Paths: Charting Courses to Success for Organizations and Their Employees
Gary W. Carter, Kevin W. Cook and David W. Dorsey

Mistreatment in the Workplace: Prevention and Resolution for Managers and Organizations
Julie B. Olson-Buchanan and Wendy R. Boswell

Developing Women Leaders: A Guide for Men and Women in Organizations
Anna Marie Valerio

Employee Engagement: Tools for Analysis, Practice, and Competitive Advantage
William H. Macey, Benjamin Schneider, Karen M. Barbera, and Scott A. Young

Online Recruiting and Selection: Innovations in Talent Acquisition
Douglas H. Reynolds and John Weiner

Senior Executive Assessment: A Key to Responsible Corporate Governance
Dean Stamoulis

Real-Time Leadership Development
Paul R. Yost and Mary Mannion Plunkett

Performance Management

A New Approach for Driving Business Results

Elaine D. Pulakos

WILEY-BLACKWELL

A John Wiley & Sons, Ltd., Publication

This edition first published 2009
© 2009 Elaine D. Pulakos

Blackwell Publishing was acquired by John Wiley & Sons in February 2007. Blackwell's publishing program has been merged with Wiley's global Scientific, Technical, and Medical business to form Wiley-Blackwell.

Registered Office
John Wiley & Sons Ltd, The Atrium, Southern Gate, Chichester, West Sussex, PO19 8SQ, United Kingdom

Editorial Offices
350 Main Street, Malden, MA 02148-5020, USA
9600 Garsington Road, Oxford, OX4 2DQ, UK
The Atrium, Southern Gate, Chichester, West Sussex, PO19 8SQ, UK

For details of our global editorial offices, for customer services, and for information about how to apply for permission to reuse the copyright material in this book please see our website at www.wiley.com/wiley-blackwell.

The right of Elaine D. Pulakos to be identified as the author of this work has been asserted in accordance with the Copyright, Designs and Patents Act 1988.

Wiley also publishes its books in a variety of electronic formats. Some content that appears in print may not be available in electronic books.

Designations used by companies to distinguish their products are often claimed as trademarks. All brand names and product names used in this book are trade names, service marks, trademarks or registered trademarks of their respective owners. The publisher is not associated with any product or vendor mentioned in this book. This publication is designed to provide accurate and authoritative information in regard to the subject matter covered. It is sold on the understanding that the publisher is not engaged in rendering professional services. If professional advice or other expert assistance is required, the services of a competent professional should be sought.

Library of Congress Cataloging-in-Publication Data

Pulakos, Elaine Diane.
  Performance management : a new approach for driving business results / Elaine D. Pulakos.
    p. cm. – (Talent management essentials)
  Includes bibliographical references and index.
  ISBN 978-1-4051-7762-7 (hardcover : alk. paper) – ISBN 978-1-4051-7761-0 (pbk. : alk. paper)
  1. Performance–Management.   2. Performance standards.   3. Personnel management.   I. Title.
  HF5549.5.P35P848 2009
  658.4′013–dc22

2008032197

A catalogue record for this book is available from the British Library.
Icon in Case Scenario boxes © Kathy Konkle/istockphoto.com.

Set in 10.5/12.5 pt Minion by SNP Best-set Typesetter Ltd., Hong Kong

Contents

Series Editor's Preface

The *Talent Management Essentials* series presents state-of-the-art thinking on critical talent management topics ranging from global staffing, to career pathing, to engagement, to executive staffing, to performance management, to mentoring, to real-time leadership development. Authored by leading authorities and scholars on their respective topics, each volume offers state-of-the-art thinking and the epitome of evidence-based practice. These authors bring to their books an incredible wealth of experience working with small, large, public and private organizations, as well as keen insights into the science and best practices associated with talent management.

Written succinctly and without superfluous "fluff," this series provides powerful and practical treatments of essential talent topics critical to maximizing individual and organizational health, well-being and effectiveness. The books, taken together, provide a comprehensive and contemporary treatment of approaches, tools, and techniques associated with Talent Management. The goal of the series is to produce focused, prescriptive volumes that translate the data- and practice-based knowledge of I/O psychology and Organizational Behavior into practical, "how to" advice for dealing with cutting-edge organizational issues and problems.

Talent Management Essentials is a comprehensive, practitioner-oriented series of "best practices" for the busy solution-oriented manager, executive, HR leader, and consultant. And, in its application of evidence-based practice, this series will also appeal to professors, executive MBA students, and graduate students in Organizational Behavior, Human Resources Management, and I/O Psychology.

Steven Rogelberg

Preface

While there are many books on effective performance management systems and practices, many have focused on the development of competencies and behavioral performance measures, which have been the focus of performance management for some time. The newest trend in performance management is "results-oriented" performance management systems that use cascading goals to align individual efforts with organizational strategy and goals. Although it is impossible to find fault with the idea that results-oriented performance management makes sense, there is very little information, guidance, and best practices available to guide implementation of these types of systems. Furthermore, as human resources professionals are attempting to implement these systems, they are quickly realizing that there are significant challenges associated with them, such as how to effectively define specific goals where some jobs are very fluid and ever changing or have rote performance requirements; how to ensure fairness when some managers set very hard target goals and others easy target goals, especially when goal accomplishment is linked to pay; and how to put contributions from goal attainment on a scale so that you can systematically and fairly evaluate and properly reward people who deliver different types of results.

This book presents an end-to-end practical, proven, and effective performance management solution that focuses on achieving important results that lead to organizational effectiveness and also on driving effective employee behavior. The focus on both results and behavior is important because the most impressive results fade in the presence of bad behavior, just as the presence of effective behavior (e.g, positive teamwork, effective interpersonal skills) does not mean much without accompanying results.

Although tips for driving effective behaviors at work are discussed, the key contribution is development and implementation of performance management systems that lead to important results based on cascading goals from the organizational level down to the individual employee. Particular emphasis will be given to the circumstances and types of jobs where this approach works best and those where it doesn't. Practical advice and examples are provided throughout the book, translating best practices, ideas, and concepts into concrete and practical development and implementation steps that human capital professionals and managers can apply in their own work situations.

Part I

A Primer on Performance Management

Chapter 1

The Truth about Performance Management

Performance management is known as the "Achilles' Heel" of human capital management, and it is the most difficult HR system to implement in organizations.

Important data from Watson Wyatt:

- Only 30% of workers felt their company's performance management system helps them improve their performance.
- Less than 40% said their systems provide clear performance goals, generate honest feedback, or use technology effectively.

In fact, performance management is consistently one of the lowest, if not the lowest, rated area in employee satisfaction surveys. Yet, performance management is the key process through which work gets done. It's how organizations communicate expectations and drive behavior to achieve important goals; it's also how organizations identify ineffective performers for development programs or other personnel actions.

> **Given the critical role of performance management and its inherent challenges, this book provides . . .**
>
> - Time-proven methods, down-to-earth tips, and nuts-and-bolts advice for designing and implementing a successful performance management system, explained in the context of practical realities.
> - Real-life examples to help negotiate the obstacles and organizational barriers faced when implementing performance management.
> - Training exercises and example tools, complete with forms and procedures needed to build a fair, effective, and high impact performance management system.

What Makes Performance Management So Hard?

There are genuine reasons why both managers and employees have difficulties with performance management. Managers avoid performance management activities, especially providing developmental feedback to employees, because they don't want to risk damaging relationships with the very individuals they count on to get work done. Employees avoid performance management activities, especially discussing their development needs with managers, because they don't want to jeopardize their pay or advancement. In addition, many employees feel that their managers are unskilled at discussing their performance and coaching them on how to improve. These attitudes, on the part of both managers and employees, result in poor performance management processes that simply don't work well.

Another problem is that many managers and employees don't understand the benefits of effective performance management. They often view it as a paperwork drill required by human resources, where ratings need to be submitted on a yearly basis for record-keeping purposes – a necessary evil that warrants the minimum investment of time. What many managers don't realize is that performance management is the most important tool they have for getting work done. It's essential for high performing organizations, and one of their most important responsibilities. Done correctly, performance management communicates what's important to the organization, drives employees to achieve important goals, and implements the organization's strategy.

On the other hand, done poorly, performance management has significant negative consequences for organizations, managers, and employees. Managers who conduct performance management ineffectively will not only fail to realize its benefits, but they can

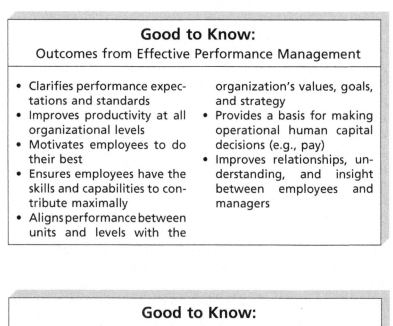

Good to Know:
Outcomes from Effective Performance Management

- Clarifies performance expectations and standards
- Improves productivity at all organizational levels
- Motivates employees to do their best
- Ensures employees have the skills and capabilities to contribute maximally
- Aligns performance between units and levels with the organization's values, goals, and strategy
- Provides a basis for making operational human capital decisions (e.g., pay)
- Improves relationships, understanding, and insight between employees and managers

Good to Know:
Outcomes from Ineffective Performance Management

- Decreases productivity and motivation
- Undermines employee confidence
- May cause employees to quit their jobs as a result of how they are treated
- Fails to develop skills and capabilities employees need to contribute maximally
- Damages relationships between employees and managers
- Wastes time and money on training and a host of support activities
- Makes it impossible to meaningfully link rewards to performance outcomes
- Can result in legal challenges and significant problems for organizations

damage relationships with or undermine the self-confidence of their employees. If employees do not feel they are being treated fairly, they become de-motivated, or worse, they may legally challenge the organization's performance management practices. This can result in serious problems that are expensive, distracting, and damaging to an organization's reputation and functioning.

The Goal of This Book

At some level of formality, performance management exists in every organization. Because it is such a vital part of organizational functioning, this book provides practical advice to leaders, human resources professionals, managers, and employees about how to achieve the maximum benefits from performance management. Although the book centers on design and implementation of performance management systems, many of the topics are relevant to individual managers and employees who are trying to get the most from their own performance management activities.

The approach offered here focuses on using performance management to achieve important business outcomes through driving effective employee results and behaviors. It is based on best practices that have evolved from research and lessons learned from implementing performance management in many diverse organizations. While many of the general ideas and best practices discussed here are not new, what is new is how these are combined into the recommended performance management process and steps and, most important, the focus on what it really takes to implement the best practices so that performance management adds value, achieves its goals, and produces results.

So often, when people think about performance management, the basic process and tools seem so straightforward and easy to implement that they miss what it really takes to gain value and results from a performance management process. What happens is that "flavor of the day" performance management practices are enthusiastically and readily adopted, without considering their fit within the given organizational context – specifically, whether the infrastructure and support are there for successful implementation. The reality is that best practices should not be automatically adopted just because someone has christened them as such. Instead, performance management needs to be designed in light of the climate for, commitment to, and desired outcomes from performance management in a given organization. In the end, the best-designed tools mean nothing if organizational members do not believe in the value of performance management and use performance management processes effectively. Therefore, it is critically important to assess the particular circumstances within an organization, be realistic about what can be achieved in a given situation, and then implement performance management processes that make the most sense.

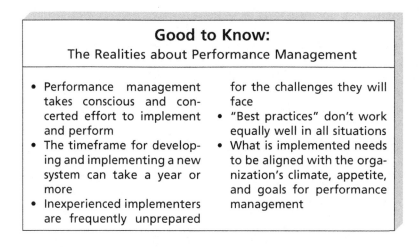

Good to Know:
The Realities about Performance Management

- Performance management takes conscious and concerted effort to implement and perform
- The timeframe for developing and implementing a new system can take a year or more
- Inexperienced implementers are frequently unprepared for the challenges they will face
- "Best practices" don't work equally well in all situations
- What is implemented needs to be aligned with the organization's climate, appetite, and goals for performance management

In light of the truth about performance management, the remainder of this book:

- provides a roadmap and practical steps for developing results-oriented performance management processes that actually work
- helps you understand what it *really* takes to implement best practices successfully in your organization, and importantly
- shows you how to determine which performance management options will be the most successful in your situation.

The book is divided into three parts. Part I contains *introductory information* and includes this chapter and the next, which provide a brief history of performance management that explains how today's best practices evolved. Part II focuses on the performance management *process* – what questions need to be addressed, what steps need to be included, and how to implement performance management systems successfully. Part III provides nuts and bolts guidance on how to develop effective performance *measures*.

Chapter 2

How Did We Arrive at Today's Best Practices?

Today's performance management best practices are the result of ongoing efforts to address two key challenges that have plagued performance measurement since its inception:

- What type of performance should be measured – abilities, skills, behaviors, results?
- How can we measure performance most reliably, accurately, and fairly?

To understand where we are today with performance management and why certain approaches have become best practices, you need to understand how they evolved over time, based on trial and error.

The start was defining rating standards...
- The beginning of formal performance management can be attributed to principles of "scientific management," developed by industrial engineers in the early 1900s. These principles emphasized the importance of defining standards against which to measure performance,[1] an important best practice today.

Next, abilities were evaluated...
- During World War I (1914–1918), the performance of Army officers was evaluated, with a focus on assessing officer ability.[2] These efforts marked the first large-scale use of judgmental assessment

and began to solidify the use of performance management systems in government and industry.

Scales were developed to measure job-relevant traits . . .
- In 1922, the Graphic Rating Scale was introduced.[3] This scale was designed to elicit ratings of traits relevant to a job and was anchored with verbal anchors, numerical anchors, or both. Use of a rating scale was a significant step forward. However, one problem with graphic rating scales was that the rating points were not well defined. For example, a scale might have assessed whether an employee "Exceeded," "Met," or "Failed to Meet" expectations, without articulating exactly what those expectations were. This left managers to develop their own interpretations of the rating scale points. Since some managers inevitably expect more than others. The result was that employees were held to different standards. Thus, graphic rating scales were limited because they did not provide sufficiently defined standards that managers could use to systematically and fairly evaluate employees. The problem of sufficiently defining performance standards to guide evaluations has continued to plague performance management.[4]

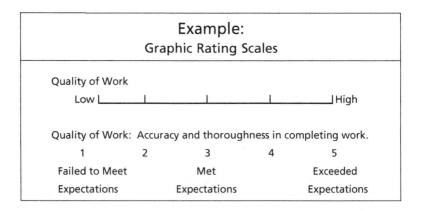

Example:
Graphic Rating Scales

Quality of Work

Low |_____|_____|_____|_____| High

Quality of Work: Accuracy and thoroughness in completing work.

1	2	3	4	5
Failed to Meet		Met		Exceeded
Expectations		Expectations		Expectations

Performance measurement evolved to assess work outcomes and behaviors . . .
- In the 1950s and 1960s, there was development and expansion of the types of performance rated, beyond job relevant traits.[5,6] This happened because it was recognized that traits (e.g., conscientiousness), thought to underlie job performance, were not the most

direct and meaningful thing to evaluate. As a result, attention shifted to more direct and observable measures of performance. These included both objective outcome measures (e.g., dollar volume of sales) and subjective (e.g., behavioral) measures. For example, in 1954, a behavioral measure, called the critical incident technique, was introduced by Flanagan.[7] This technique focused on eliciting specific examples of effective and ineffective job behaviors and moved performance measurement away from traits towards observable behavior.

Objectives-based performance measures took center-stage . . .
- Also in 1954, Management by Objectives (MBO) was introduced by Peter Drucker in his book, *The Practice of Management*. MBO involves defining concrete and specific objectives so that both managers and employees understand what the employee is expected to achieve. MBO systems increased in their popularity and use, particularly in the 1970s. However, experience with MBO revealed several difficulties, including the time it took to set measurable objectives for each and every employee, unforeseen events that required objectives to be continually modified throughout the rating period, and defining objectives that were entirely within the employee's control. These difficulties led many organizations to abandon the MBO approach to performance management.

Behavior-based performance measures took center-stage . . .
- The trend increasingly moved more towards measuring job behavior, including the development of pre-defined behavioral standards against which employees could be evaluated. Assessing job behavior circumvented the problems associated with measuring objectives – that they often needed to be revised during the rating period, accomplishing objectives can be influenced by things outside an employee's control, and considerable time is required to define individual, customized objectives for each employee. A major influencing force was the development of Behaviorally Anchored Rating Scales (BARS) in the early 1960s, which focused on quantifying behavioral job performance.[8] These scales focused on assessing performance dimensions that represent the major job requirements (Figure 2.1). Within each dimension, specific behaviors anchor different rating levels, as shown in the example on p. 10. These behaviors provide managers with concrete examples

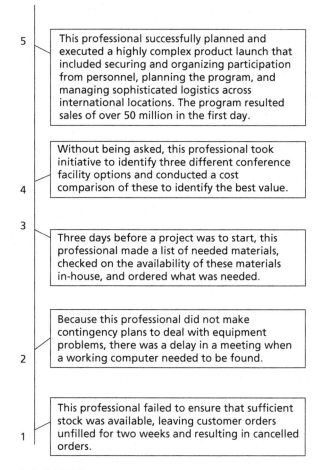

5 | This professional successfully planned and executed a highly complex product launch that included securing and organizing participation from personnel, planning the program, and managing sophisticated logistics across international locations. The program resulted sales of over 50 million in the first day.

Without being asked, this professional took initiative to identify three different conference facility options and conducted a cost comparison of these to identify the best value.
4

3

Three days before a project was to start, this professional made a list of needed materials, checked on the availability of these materials in-house, and ordered what was needed.

Because this professional did not make contingency plans to deal with equipment problems, there was a delay in a meeting when a working computer needed to be found.
2

This professional failed to ensure that sufficient stock was available, leaving customer orders unfilled for two weeks and resulting in cancelled orders.
1

Figure 2.1 BARS Format

Example: More General Behavioral Anchors for Work Planning Competency		
1 **2**	**3**	**4** **5**
Fails to Meet Expectations	**Meets Expectations**	**Exceeds Expectations**
Fails to prioritize work for self or others to ensure timely completion of projects and assignments. Does not anticipate or take steps to mitigate obstacles that impact work schedule or delivery.	Independently prioritizes, plans, organizes, and schedules own work activities to ensure assignments are completed in a timely manner. Coordinates work activities with coworkers and work unit; takes initiative to keep others informed of progress, problems, or changes. Sees obvious problems and makes recommendations to overcome them so that progress is not impeded.	**"Meets Expectations" plus does the following:** Demonstrates a high level of skill in complex planning to include coordination across organizational units, multiple facilities, and solving thorny logistical problems, resulting in contributions far beyond what is expected at this level. Takes initiative to help others plan efforts for the group to ensure goals are met. Anticipates important roadblocks and takes effective preemptive action to prevent them, ensuring effective progress on projects.

of the type of performance that is associated with different effectiveness levels.

Behavior-based performance measures improved . . .

- The BARS rating format was an important step in developing well-defined rating scales. However, one limitation of these scales was that it could be difficult to match an employee's performance to the very specific behavioral examples used to anchor the rating scale.[9] Even though an employee might be performing at a level represented by an example behavior, the employee probably would not have exhibited the exact behavior that appears on the scale. This required managers to infer which of the few scaled behaviors best matched an employee's performance. Several variants of the behaviorally-based method followed in the late 1970s and early 1980s to address this issue.[10,11] Rather than using only a few very specific behaviors to anchor the rating scale points, more general behavioral descriptions were used to anchor different effectiveness levels. The use of more general behavioral descriptions made it easier for managers to match their observations of employee performance to a rating scale point. Today, well-defined behavioral standards remain a hallmark of effective performance management systems.

Civil rights put a focus on fairness . . .

- The civil rights movement of the late 1950s and early 1960s drew attention to the fact that minorities had systematically been denied equal opportunity in areas such as housing, education, and employment. The Civil Rights Act of 1964 and subsequent legislation was passed to rectify these inequities and prohibited discrimination in employment practices. Performance appraisals, which often serve as the basis for pay, promotions, and terminations, were required to be job-relevant. This requirement was reiterated in 1979 with the publication of the EEOC *Uniform Guidelines on Employee Selection Procedures.*[12] The implication of this legislation was that certain procedures to ensure job relevance needed to be followed in developing performance management systems. For more guidance on these procedures, see the Society for Industrial and Organizational

Psychology's, *Principles for the validation and use of personnel selection procedures.*[13]

Multi-source ratings gained popularity . . .

- Developing out of work in the 1940s,[14] the 1960s and 1970s saw an increased focus on gathering performance information from rating sources other than managers, such as peers and customers.[15] The idea behind collecting performance information from different sources is that, depending on one's relationship to the employee, he or she will see different aspects of performance. For example, a customer is probably in the best position to judge someone's customer service skills. Likewise, a direct report will see aspects of performance dealing with providing feedback and mentoring that an individual's manager may never directly observe. In the early 1990s, formal multi-source or 360-degree feedback programs further evolved out of organizational trends such as employee involvement, self-managed work teams, and an increased focus on customer satisfaction. These programs quickly gained widespread popularity in the workplace.[16]

Competencies took center-stage . . .

- Through the 1990s and into the 2000s, organizations have increasingly adopted competency-based human capital systems, including the use of competency models as the basis for performance management.[17] Although extremely popular, there has been debate about what "competencies" are and how to most effectively measure them. Sometimes, competencies reflect knowledge areas and skills, sometimes they reflect performance factors, sometimes they reflect values, and sometimes they reflect personality traits. Here, competencies are defined as the knowledge, skills, abilities, and other personal characteristics that are most instrumental for achieving important job outcomes that contribute to organizational success (Figure 2.2). A best practice in the use of competencies for performance management purposes has been defining them in terms of behavioral performance standards that describe different levels of effectiveness in each competency area.

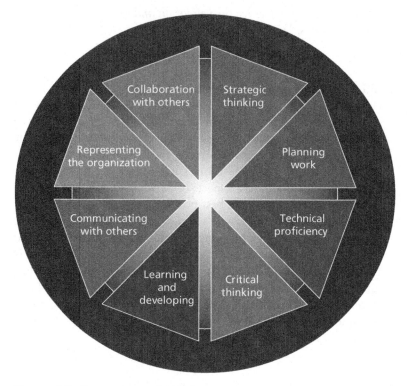

Figure 2.2 Competency Model

Results became the bottom line . . .
- The most recent trend in performance management is incorporation of a "results-focus."[18] The emergence of this trend is largely due to organizations becoming increasingly focused on achieving results, not just driving effective behaviors. The idea is that each employee needs to be accountable for producing results that contribute to the organization achieving its goals.[19] It has thus become best practice today to assess both the results employees achieve as well as how they went about achieving these – or in other words, their job behavior.

Part II

How to Design and Implement a Successful Performance Management Process

Chapter 3

Getting Started

When people think about implementing a performance manage-ment system, some of the first things that come to mind are developing a competency model, selecting an automated tool, and, importantly, determining how quickly the new system can be ready for use. What people sometimes underestimate or don't realize at all is how much of a shock a new performance management system can be to organizational members. They are surprised by:

- How much employees sometimes fight against or undermine a new system
- How much emotion is generated
- How much effort is needed to get everyone on-board with a new system.

This is especially true when the system involves major changes that are threatening to employees, such as linking performance manage-ment to pay. Before thinking about the details of the performance management system itself, two important decisions need to be made and three steps are necessary to lay the groundwork for a new system.

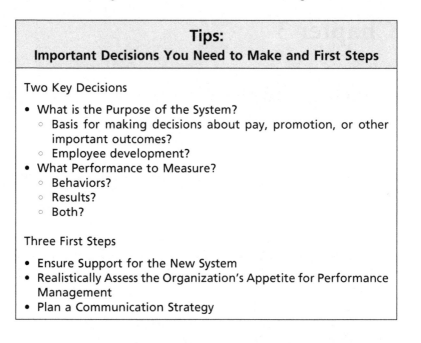

Tips:

Important Decisions You Need to Make and First Steps

Two Key Decisions

- What is the Purpose of the System?
  - Basis for making decisions about pay, promotion, or other important outcomes?
  - Employee development?
- What Performance to Measure?
  - Behaviors?
  - Results?
  - Both?

Three First Steps

- Ensure Support for the New System
- Realistically Assess the Organization's Appetite for Performance Management
- Plan a Communication Strategy

What Is the Purpose of the System?

Many organizations use their performance management system as a basis for decision-making, such as pay, bonuses, promotions, assignments, and reductions in force. Other, but fewer, organizations use their performance management systems to guide employee development. This means using performance information as a basis for development planning to help employees enhance their skills. Neither decision-making nor development is an unequivocally better use of a performance management system. Both purposes have their advantages and disadvantages. However, one or the other purpose is usually better fit for the goals and circumstances in a given organization.

Tips:
How to Decide if Decision-Making or Development Makes Most Sense

Performance Management for Decision-Making (e.g., pay) Makes Sense when:	Performance Management for Development Makes Sense when
• There are significant, contingent rewards available to employees • There is a goal to drive high impact and significant results through performance management • There is a desire for strong and explicit ties between performance and rewards	• Pay decisions are more tenure-based than performance-based, for instance, as in many civil service settings • There is not much differential pay, pay that can be put at risk, or other meaningful rewards that are available

While use of performance management for decision-making or development is more appropriate in certain situations, it is extremely difficult, if not impossible, to serve both purposes equally well with the same system.[1] An example will show why.

Case Scenario:
Why Decision-Making and Development Goals Can't Be Easily Achieved with One System

In an information technology organization, employees' pay and stock options were tied to performance. Although development was supposed to be included in the process, the range of pay increases and stock options was large, allowing managers to make very meaningful links between performance and rewards. With so much at stake, both managers and employees were most concerned with justifying rewards. The decision-making consequences of performance management were, by default, given much more emphasis than development.[2]

For a performance management system to achieve its maximum benefit, it is best to choose one purpose – decision-making or development – and then develop the system to support that purpose. In many organizations, however, there is a precedent for using performance management systems for both decision-making and development purposes. In these situations, one option is to break up the two uses by first having a decision-making review and then having a developmental discussion at a later point in time, or vice versa. This can help to avoid some of the problems inherent in trying to discuss decisions and development at the same time. One caveat is that managers and staff often perceive it as burdensome to have two formal review sessions for these different purposes, and it can be difficult to ensure that both discussions actually happen. Nonetheless, in situations where a system is used for both purposes, encouraging split discussions for decision-making versus development is the most productive strategy.

Best Practices and Realities:
Purpose of Performance Management

Best Practice

- Select one primary purpose for performance management – decision-making or development, because both purposes cannot be served equally well with one system

Realities

- Many organizations already use their performance management system for both decision-making and development
- Helps to physically separate outcome discussion from development discussion, conducting these at two separate points in time

---

In situations where it is possible to make a decision about the purpose of the system upfront, there are consequences of this that are important to understand. First, the purpose of appraisal affects the variability of the ratings managers provide.[3] Ratings that are used for decision-making tend to be more lenient than ratings used for development. This means that most employees receive ratings at the high end of the rating scale, and there are fewer differences in the ratings received by different employees. The reason why managers rate their employees at the high end of the scale is that they do not want to jeopardize the rewards that are available to their employees. If there are fixed pools of money, which there always are, managers worry about how their ratings will stack up against other managers' ratings. For example, if one manager's ratings reflect employees' strengths and development needs but another manager's only reflect strengths, employees working for the first manager may well end up with smaller raises or bonuses than those working for the second. As a result, when rewards are tied to evaluation outcomes, managers tend to provide ratings of their employees that will compare favorably against the ratings given by other managers. When all managers end up doing this, the ratings of all employees across the board are driven upward.

Alternatively, ratings that are used strictly for development purposes tend to be for employees' own benefit – to help them understand their strengths and address performance gaps. In this situation, there are essentially no negative consequences associated with identifying development areas, particularly when the expectation is that these will be identified for all employees. As a result, ratings used strictly for development purposes tend to be more variable, better reflecting employee strengths and development needs.

While the purpose of the performance management system should be based on the organization's performance management goals, this decision has implications for several system design decisions.

What Type of Rating Will Be Made?

If performance management is used for decision-making, numerical ratings are essential. This is because a numerical score is needed to order employees to guide decision-making. Decisions cannot be made in a systematic or fair manner based on unstructured narratives. Also, it is difficult to make meaningful decisions based on categorical ratings, such as "pass or fail" or Exceeds, Meets, or Fails to Meet Expectations, because these don't provide much differentiation between employees. For example, everyone who receives a "pass" (or "fail") would need to be given the exact same pay, promotion, etc. Evaluation of multiple dimensions or competencies using a five- or

Good to Know:
Implications of Deciding to Use a System for
Decision-Making or Development

System Design Decisions	If Used for Decision-Making	If Used for Development
What type of rating will be made?	Numerical ratings better	Categorical, non-numerical ratings better
Will managers provide narratives to support ratings?	Numerical ratings essential but narratives can provide useful information to justify ratings – caveat is that narratives must fully support and align with numerical ratings	Narratives essential and more important than numerical ratings, because they help employees more fully understand their strengths and development needs
Will performance information be provided by multiple rating sources or the manager alone?	Manager needs to serve a gatekeeper function, interpreting and integrating information from others	Not necessary for manager to provide final ratings; ratings from different sources can be fed back directly to recipients
Will processes be included for managers to calibrate their ratings?	Very important	Not important

seven-point rating scale is the best strategy for achieving sufficient distinctions between employees to make sound decisions about pay, promotion, and so forth.

If a system is used strictly for development, there is less need for numerical ratings. In fact, these often detract from development. This is because numerical ratings cause employees to be more concerned about their "score" and the message it sends than understanding their development needs. Rather than use numerical ratings, many development systems use categorical ratings to identify whether a rating dimension or competency "is a development area" or "is not a development area." Sometimes more differentiated categories are used to set development priorities, such as:

- Development Need for Current Job
- Development Need for Career Progression
- Not a Development Need

Will Managers Provide Narratives to Support Ratings?

From a development perspective, narratives provide more useful information than numerical ratings. Even when performance is rated against defined standards, ratings do not convey exactly what the employee did in sufficient detail to fully explain the rating or provide meaningful feedback. Alternatively, narratives can be rich, customized, and useful sources of feedback, because they usually provide context and examples that aid employees in understanding the rationale for their ratings. Narrative descriptions also help managers calibrate their ratings (discussed below) by providing specific examples of behavior that can be discussed with other managers to ensure they are all applying the performance standards in a similar way.

While narratives can facilitate decision-making, they should not be used alone as a basis for decisions. Without accompanying standards and numerical ratings, narratives tend to be unstructured, unstandardized, and can reflect the motivation and writing skills of the manager more than the performance of the employee. Further, it is extremely difficult to rank order employees or assign rewards based on narratives alone. One caveat is that care must be taken to ensure that rating narratives support the numerical ratings. If this is not the case, employees will, at a minimum, be confused by their evaluation or worse, they may have grounds for challenging their ratings.

Will Information Come from Multiple Rating Sources or Only the Manager?

Because managers, peers, direct reports, and customers see different aspects of a person's performance, multi-source assessments offer an effective and credible way to obtain feedback. When multiple raters are involved, the manager is no longer the sole judge of performance. This allows the manager to assume more of a coaching and mentoring role, helping to interpret the feedback and plan development steps. When multi-source assessments are used, it is important to collect ratings from at least three raters of each type (e.g., peers, direct reports). This helps to protect the anonymity of individual raters, which is important for obtaining accurate and useful feedback.[4,5] Particularly in the case of direct reports and peers, feedback providers do not want to risk damaging relationships if their feedback is not appreciated by the receiver. Additionally, individuals representing rating sources other than the manager (e.g., peers, direct reports) often are not experienced in making performance ratings. The use of at least three raters from each source helps to ensure that more reliable feedback results from the process.

If performance ratings will be used for decision-making, managers should provide the final evaluations. While managers should gather and consider information from other sources, it is important that they serve as gate-keepers, judging its credibility and quality, and balancing it against other available information. This is important because raters from different sources often do not have the experience, perspective, or motivation to make accurate ratings. In fact, research has shown decrements in the quality of multi-source ratings when they are used for decision-making versus development.[6]

Will Processes Be Included for Managers to Calibrate Their Ratings?

Rating calibration is a process where managers get together within a business unit or function to discuss their ratings of employees and

Case Scenario:
How Decision-Making Can Undermine
Multi-Source Ratings

After using a multi-source rating program strictly for development purposes, a financial services organization was considering changing focus and using the multi-source ratings for decision-making. Wisely, the organization first conducted a pilot study in two departments to evaluate whether or not there would be any impact on the ratings. Evaluation of the pilot study ratings showed many more positive ratings than when the system used for development only. Compromises to the ratings were also discovered. For example, in anonymous interviews, peers reported cutting deals to exchange one good appraisal for another, when they thought multi-source ratings would be used for decision-making. Additionally, some customers reported that they were asked to discuss any areas of dissatisfaction privately and directly with employees rather then reflecting these in their multi-source evaluations. Based on these findings, the organization decided to retain the multi-source program for development only.

identify areas where they may have inadvertently applied different standards. Even when a rating system contains well-defined rating standards, each manager may still interpret those standards somewhat differently. For example, when deciding whether a project was of moderate or high complexity, one manager may come to a very different conclusion than another. By discussing more specific details and examples of performance, managers develop more similar views of how to interpret and apply the standards, resulting in ratings that are more systematic and fair across employees. In performance management systems that are used for decision-making, it is important for managers to calibrate their ratings to ensure similar standards are applied. In development systems, rating calibration is useful but not as important.

What Performance to Measure?

There are differences of opinion about what should be measured – behaviors, results, or both? Behavioral assessments focus on identifying the most critical dimensions or competencies that are required to perform effectively on a job (e.g., Communication, Critical Thinking, Managing Resources, Planning and Organizing, etc.) and defining behavioral standards that describe levels of performance effectiveness in these. The standards help managers match their observations of employee performance to an appropriate rating level in each area.

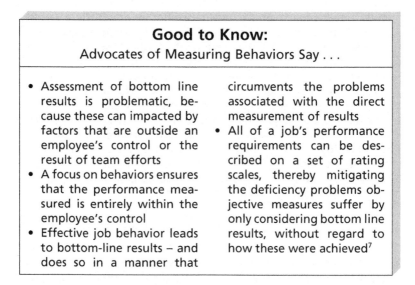

Good to Know:
Advocates of Measuring Behaviors Say . . .

- Assessment of bottom line results is problematic, because these can impacted by factors that are outside an employee's control or the result of team efforts
- A focus on behaviors ensures that the performance measured is entirely within the employee's control
- Effective job behavior leads to bottom-line results – and does so in a manner that circumvents the problems associated with the direct measurement of results
- All of a job's performance requirements can be described on a set of rating scales, thereby mitigating the deficiency problems objective measures suffer by only considering bottom line results, without regard to how these were achieved[7]

Opponents of the behavioral-only view feel that an exclusive focus on behaviors is remiss in not sufficiently emphasizing results that contribute to an organization's success. Organizations have long been driven by bottom-line results. This focus has only continued to increase in recent years, especially in light of intense national and international competition. This "results focus" has not only affected private sector organizations but a similar trend has been observed in public sector and not-for-profit organizations, as well – organizations that traditionally have not been driven by bottom-line results. As examples:

• To better compete in their market, IBM underwent performance-based restructuring in the 1990s.

- Also in the 1990s, the Internal Revenue Service (IRS), Federal Aviation Administration (FAA), and Government Accountability Office (GAO) all initiated performance management systems that focused on achieving key business results.
- Recently, the U.S. Departments of Defense (DoD) and Homeland Security (DHS) have implemented similar results-oriented performance management programs.

The value of focusing on results and using these to drive performance has been a cornerstone of many performance management trends, at least as far back as the MBO systems that were popular in the 1970s.[8]

Good to Know:
Advocates of Measuring Results Say . . .

- Measuring behaviors misses what's really essential – whether the individual delivered important bottom-line results
- Employees can engage in highly effective behaviors and never deliver results

- Employees need specific goals and expectations that let them know what specific results they are accountable for

---

Although results-oriented approaches to performance management are intuitively appealing, an exclusive focus on results can, in fact, yield a deficient performance assessment because little or no consideration is given to *how* employees go about achieving their results.[9] While one can achieve impressive results, performance is not effective if individuals are extremely difficult to work with, unhelpful, or cause problems. However, it is also the case that an employee can be extremely helpful, considerate, and interpersonally effective, yet never get anything important accomplished. While an organization can choose to focus exclusively on results or behaviors, many have opted to include both because comprehensive performance assessment should consider what someone has achieved (their results) as well as how they went about achieving these (their job behavior). In

Chapters 7 and 8, strategies are provided for effectively defining and measuring both results and behaviors that circumvent some of the challenges associated with each type of measure.

Ensure Support for the New System

For a performance management system to be effective, organizational members must accept it, believe it is worth their time, and be motivated to use it. Research on implementing many different types of organizational programs clearly shows that success depends, first, on top management support for the program. The stronger the leadership commitment, the greater the system's success will be.[10] Without management support, the system will fail.

What's needed for effective implementation of performance management is a committed CEO who believes in its benefits, engages in effective performance management practices, and makes all employees accountable for doing the same. One particularly effective CEO in an auditing organization demonstrated his commitment to the performance management system by communicating extensively about the importance of performance management, modeling effective performance management behavior with his direct reports, and

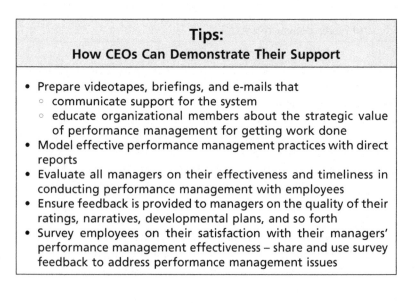

Tips:
How CEOs Can Demonstrate Their Support

- Prepare videotapes, briefings, and e-mails that
  - communicate support for the system
  - educate organizational members about the strategic value of performance management for getting work done
- Model effective performance management practices with direct reports
- Evaluate all managers on their effectiveness and timeliness in conducting performance management with employees
- Ensure feedback is provided to managers on the quality of their ratings, narratives, developmental plans, and so forth
- Survey employees on their satisfaction with their managers' performance management effectiveness – share and use survey feedback to address performance management issues

making effective performance management a critical evaluation element in all managers' appraisals. This CEO's obvious commitment to performance management through both his words and deeds resulted in the organization having a highly effective performance management process that was taken seriously and shown to drive important organizational metrics.

Some organizations will already have a strong performance management culture where top management understands its value and uses it effectively. In others, it may be necessary to educate the executive team on the critical role that performance management plays in helping organizations achieve their goals. They may also need to be educated on their critical role in leading the effort. Piloting a new system with executive or leadership teams can be a useful strategy for gaining the support of these individuals. In situations where there is not a strong performance management culture, it can be established over time. However, it is not wise to proceed with implementation until leadership support has been secured.

For a performance management system to gain support, people must see it as a process that helps them achieve their goals. If leaders do not view performance management as an important strategic tool for accomplishing their goals, they will not take it seriously, devote time to it, or use it properly – consequently, it will not yield its potential benefits. One effective strategy of getting leaders on board is to show them how performance management helps drive individual behaviors and contributions that, in turn, produce results for the

---

Tips:
How to Get Leaders on Board

- Communicate about how performance management is the single most important tool for helping them get work done
- Show how performance management drives the results for which they are accountable
- Engage leaders in pilot testing the system, allowing them to ensure the system is maximally useful and efficient
- Provide support (training, coaching, facilitation) to ensure effective implementation

organization. To do this, the performance management system needs to set expectations that drive important organizational goals and measure performance on factors that are directly linked to organizational success. Showing that effective performance management drives business results gets leaders' attention and demonstrates the value of these systems.

Beyond leadership support of and belief in the value of performance management, in the end, a system's success relies on how effectively managers and employees use it. Getting organizational members on board to support a new system is essential, irrespective of whether the system will be used for decision-making or development. An effective strategy for gaining commitment to a new system is to involve members of different constituencies in the design and implementation process.[11] An organization's key constituencies usually include the major business lines or functions, different geographic locations where the organization does business, and representatives from different jobs. This advisory group, which is usually identified by management in collaboration with human resources, needs to be led by an experienced performance management expert who can successfully guide the group through the development and implementation process. There are four important functions the advisory group performs. It must do the following:

- Provide guidance representing their constituency
- Share information
- Serve as a conduit for convincing others about the merits of the new system
- Pilot test the system components

Provide Guidance Representing their Constituency

The advisory team can be used to provide input on decisions regarding system design or implementation. Since advisory group members represent different constituencies, they need to gather input from those they represent to understand the needs and desires of different groups. To the extent possible, it is best if advisory group members can come to consensus regarding significant system design issues. This helps to avoid dissatisfaction and in-fighting during the process.

Share Information

Another important role of the advisory group is to share information with the constituency they are representing. This helps to make sure organizational members are kept up to date about progress, implementation steps, and schedules. Sharing information requires iterative communications, where advisory group members exchange information between organizational members and the advisory team. The advisory group needs to be armed with briefing and other communication materials to ensure consistent information is shared across the organization.

Serve as a Conduit for Convincing Others about the Merits of the New System

Employees usually have significant concerns about how a new performance management system will affect them, especially if the system will be used as a basis for pay, promotions, reductions in workforce, and other important outcomes. Thus, insiders are needed to champion the benefits of the system and mitigate or address concerns. Advisory group members need to be personally convinced of the value of the system and trained to effectively market it to others. Because direct interactions between employees and advisory group members can have much more impact than general emails or other mass communications, these are a very important part of the strategy to sell the new system to others.

Pilot Test the System Components

The advisory group serves a final important role in helping to pilot and revise the system. Before large-scale implementation, it is wise to pilot test any new system to ensure that all aspects are working well and the right design decisions were made. One important advantage of pilot testing is that it provides a fresh perspective from people who were not intimately involved in the system design. It also provides a gauge of the reactions other organizational members are likely to have and familiarizes more people with the system prior to large-scale implementation. This broader involvement serves to communicate further about the system, ensures that it meets organizational needs, and encourages others to help implement the process properly.

Tips:
How to Get Organizational Members on Board

- Communicate about how performance management will help them better understand their expectations and goals
- Show that effective performance management results in fairer and more equitable outcomes
- Conscientiously address concerns and issues organizational members may have
- Allow organizational members input into the system design and participation in pilot testing
- Provide support (training, coaching, facilitation) to ensure effective implementation

---

Realistically Assess the Organization's Appetite for Performance Management

During the initial design, development, and pilot testing processes, sponsors of the performance management system need to continually assess the organization's appetite for performance management and make adjustments accordingly. In trying to develop the best system possible, inexperienced developers sometimes err on the side of including unsustainable requirements. A case scenario will show how this resulted in unintended negative consequences for one organization.

Case Scenario:
How the Best Intentions Can Result in Bad Consequences

In a management consulting organization, a strategic focus was defined to promote more regular performance conversations and feedback between managers and staff. As a result, the performance management implementation team decided to require formal feedback sessions between managers and staff on a quarterly basis to include interim ratings and complete narrative documentation. This essentially quadrupled the performance management requirements from what they were previously – they went from one formal evaluation and feedback session per year to four. This requirement ended up being so administratively

> burdensome that both managers and employees developed very
> negative attitudes about the new performance management
> system and it died of its own weight within the first year.

Some organizations need more formal performance management processes than others. For example, if informal feedback is regularly provided as a natural course of events, scheduled formal feedback sessions will probably be seen as burdensome and ineffective. Likewise, if an organization is a pure sales organization and cascading goals really come down to making certain revenues and profits, an elaborate and time-consuming process on this is not likely to be well received. The bottom line is that it is essential to be realistic about what performance management requirements organizational members have and will tolerate on a long-term basis. Even if there is high level support during the design and implementation process, this does not mean that time-consuming or burdensome requirements will be accepted. This is especially true if the requirements are not seen as adding value.

If there is not high level support and genuine belief in the value of performance management, it is even more important to carefully consider what users will accept when designing the system. Overall, it is better to implement a less burdensome system that people will use than a comprehensive system they will ignore. Although both managers and staff need to devote time to performance management to achieve its benefits, anything that can be done to make the process as efficient as possible (e.g., automation, predefining performance standards and objectives) should be done to maximize acceptance and use of the system.

Plan the Communication Strategy

Communication about a new performance management system should begin as early as possible, informing organizational members that revisions are planned and gathering input and feedback on desired system features. If implementation of a new system involves major changes that are threatening to employees, a comprehensive change-management strategy will be needed.[12] For example, if there was never an obvious link between performance and rewards and the new system will have an explicit one, employees may feel threatened and resist or sabotage the process. The communications and change-management process must clearly and simply explain the advantages and rationale for the new system.

Organizational members should be provided with ample opportunities to comment on the new system. Employee concerns should be addressed by providing explanations or making changes to the system. Obviously, it is not practical to make changes in response to each and every comment an employee may have. On the other hand, if many employees are voicing similar concerns, a great deal of goodwill will be generated by making changes that address these. It shows employees that their voices are being heard. Additionally, implementers should not underestimate the lengths employees will go to be heard, if they are unhappy with the direction the organization is taking and have recourse to do something about it.

Case Scenario:
The Lengths Employees Will
Go to be Heard

In one Federal agency, the decision had been made to move from essentially a tenure-based compensation system to a performance-based system where rewards would now be explicitly tied to employee contributions. Employees in this agency felt that the designers of their system were not listening to or addressing their concerns. After several failed attempts to effect changes that they felt were necessary to make the system work, employees initiated a letter-writing campaign to Congress expressing their concerns. Congressional Members intervened and work on the system was shut down for over two years until the issues could be resolved.

As part of their communications, some organizations undertake full-blown professional advertising campaigns, with marketing materials, "toys," and massive communication efforts to sell a new performance management system. The important point is understanding that extensive change-management work and communication are necessary to implement a new performance management system successfully.

Chapter 4

A Model Performance Management Process

Although performance management processes vary from organization to organization, best practice studies and professional publications show that essentially all systems contain variations of the eight steps shown in Figure 4.1. A common element of effective systems is that they contain well-articulated processes and roles for accomplishing performance management, with clear accountabilities for managers and employees. This helps ensure that employees are treated in a fair and equitable manner, which is especially important when performance management is used for decision-making.

Before discussing each step in detail, there are some important caveats about the process to recognize. It is:

Targeted to individuals, not teams
- While team performance is critical in many organizations, the predominant need and vast majority of performance management systems provide evaluations of individuals, which are required for decision-making and development. Thus, although there are needs for team-based performance management in some contexts, these will not be addressed here.

Most relevant for non-executives
- While many of the same principles discussed in this book apply to executive performance management, there are unique aspects of executive evaluation that are beyond the scope of this book.

Pulakos

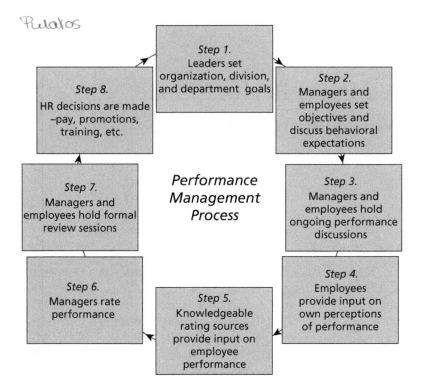

Figure 4.1 The performance management process

Not sufficient for handling disciplinary issues or serious performance problems

- While the performance management approach discussed here helps identify employees who are performing below standards, most organizations initiate a separate process with employees who consistently fail to meet standards. This involves putting employees on a formal performance improvement plan or opportunity period, where their specific deficiencies are documented, needed improvements are specified in detail, and timelines are provided within which performance targets must be met. Initiating formal opportunity periods is serious and is often a precursor to performance-based terminations. Although significant and consequential, this process falls outside of typical performance management activities and will not be treated in depth here.

The eight steps of the performance management process are discussed next, with a focus on the best practices associated with each. While the best practices oftentimes sound straightforward, they can present significant implementation challenges. Accordingly, the realities surrounding what it *really takes* to implement them well are highlighted throughout the discussion.

To illustrate important concepts concretely, examples are provided from a technology development firm's actual performance management system. The system included a competency model and results-oriented objectives for each employee. The examples that are presented focus on the job of Human Resources professional – a job that most people have encountered and understand – and the "Planning Work" and "Collaboration with Others" competencies that appear in the model in Figure 4.2.

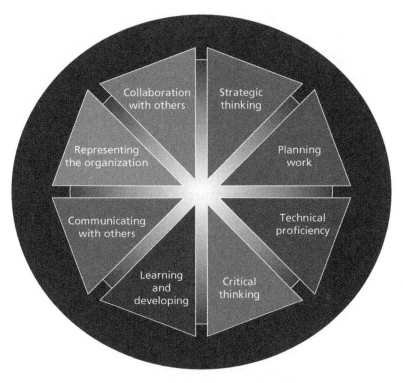

Figure 4.2 Competency model for technology development organization

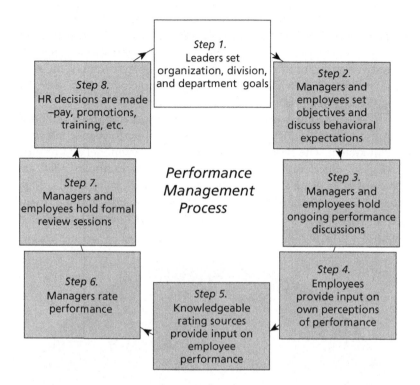

Step 1. Leaders Set Organization, Division, and Department Goals

One best practice that has been advocated recently in state-of-the-art performance management systems is to establish a hierarchy of goals where goals at each organizational level support goals directly relevant to the next level. By showing how the work performed across the organization fits together, it is more likely that everyone will be working in alignment to support the organization's strategic direction and critical priorities.[1]

Figure 4.3 shows four levels of goals, which is typical in many organizations, although there can be more or fewer levels. Looking at the connecting symbols, not every goal applies to all levels. For example, only three of the five organizational goals apply to Administrative Division. Likewise, only two of the Administrative Division's

Best Practices and Realities:
Cascading Goals

Best Practice

• Develop cascading goals where each organizational level supports goals directly relevant to the next level, ultimately working towards the organization's strategic goals and priorities

Realities

• Organizational goals are usually lofty, and it is sometimes difficult to see relationships between high level goals and what individuals do
• It is time-consuming and difficult to cascade goals through multiple organizational levels, especially the first time
• HR staff need to invest considerable time to train managers and help them identify cascading goals that are meaningful and useful as a basis for setting individual goals

goals apply to the Human Resources Department. Finally, in this example, the person's individual performance objectives support only one of the department's goals. It is extremely unlikely that an individual's performance objectives will relate to every goal at every level in the organization. What is shown in Figure 4.3 is much more typical, where an individual's objectives will support only a few higher level goals. While the value of developing and linking goals at different levels is intuitively appealing and sensible, the reality is that the process of developing cascading goals is much easier said than done.

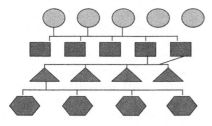

Organization ABC strategic goals

Administrative division goals

Human Resources department goals

Human resource professional's individual objectives

Figure 4.3 Cascading goals between organizational levels

One of the challenges in setting cascading goals is that it can be difficult to see relationships between high level and sometimes lofty organizational goals and the work done by individuals. To remedy this, organizational goals need to be translated into more refined goals at the division, department, and individual levels. Doing this thoughtfully and correctly is time-consuming and difficult, especially if managers are not accustomed to thinking about these linkages. As a result, the process typically requires a series of meetings:

• First, executives develop division goals that align with the organizational goals.
• Next, mid-level managers develop department goals that align with the division goals.
• Finally, department goals are cascaded down to individuals.

The bottom line is that implementation of cascading goals requires time, effort, and considerable hand-holding, at least initially, to ensure that the cascading is done well.

Case Scenario:
Developing Cascading Goals

In a retail sales organization, the organizational development (OD) group took a very active and directive role in assisting the organization in developing cascading goals. First, a consultant who had extensive performance management implementation experience was brought in to provide training to all levels of management and staff on the cascading goals process. The consultant then worked with the OD group to develop a protocol for facilitated sessions that OD staff would conduct with members of organizational units at different levels to develop cascading goals. During these sessions, the OD staff walked managers through the process, facilitated discussions to help them generate goals that linked to higher level goals, and ensured that the goals they developed would be usable by and clear to lower levels.

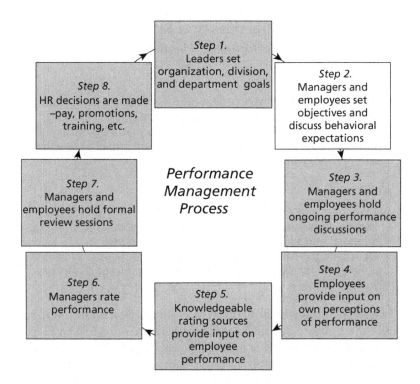

Step 2. Managers and Employees Set Objectives and Discuss Behavioral Expectations

The performance management cycle typically begins with a discussion of what is expected of employees in terms of results and behaviors. This step is important because it helps employees understand what they need to do and requires articulating evaluation standards, which increases the transparency and fairness of the process.

Behavioral and results expectations should be tied to the organization's strategic direction and goals.[2] In fact, if developed and implemented properly, performance management systems drive employees to engage in behavior and achieve results that facilitate meeting organizational goals. Behavioral expectations are frequently communicated through the use of performance standards that are aligned with the organization's core values and strategic direction. These standards are discussed with employees at the beginning of the rating cycle and used as a basis for systematically evaluating behavioral performance.

> ## Best Practices and Realities:
> ### Performance Planning
>
> ---
>
> Best Practice
>
> • Managers and employees collaboratively identify performance goals and agree on results to be achieved
> • Individual goals align with the organization's strategy and goals
> • Critical competencies and pre-defined performance standards are reviewed with employees
>
> Realities
>
> • Managers and employees experience significant difficulties in setting individual goals, so they need considerable training, support, and facilitation from HR to do this well
> • Developing meaningful, yet measurable goals that avoid the inherent difficulties with these presents significant challenges

Developing individual performance objectives is more complex. Since the aim is to define the specific results an individual employee is expected to achieve, it is difficult, except in rare circumstances, to pre-define goals that apply to more than one employee. There are also several challenges inherent in setting objectives. These include ensuring that achievement of the objective is in the employee's direct control, ensuring the result can be attributed to the employee him or herself and not a team, and ensuring that all employees in a given job and level have similarly difficult objectives. In Chapter 6, guidance is provided to help address the challenges associated with developing individual objectives.

Step 3. Managers and Employees Hold Ongoing Performance Discussions

During the performance planning process, both behavioral and results expectations should have been communicated. Performance in both of these areas should be discussed and feedback provided on an on-going basis throughout the rating period.

Regular feedback between managers and employees is particularly important concerning the performance objectives. Unforeseen cir-

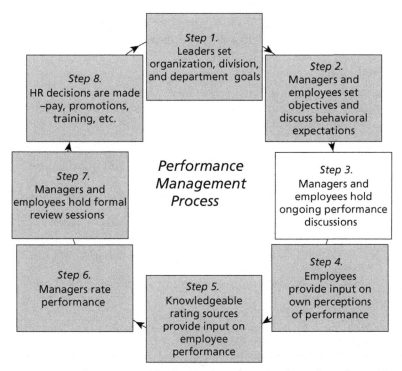

Step 1.
Leaders set organization, division, and department goals

Step 2.
Managers and employees set objectives and discuss behavioral expectations

Step 3.
Managers and employees hold ongoing performance discussions

Step 4.
Employees provide input on own perceptions of performance

Step 5.
Knowledgeable rating sources provide input on employee performance

Step 6.
Managers rate performance

Step 7.
Managers and employees hold formal review sessions

Step 8.
HR decisions are made –pay, promotions, training, etc.

Performance Management Process

cumstances that are outside an employee's control can interfere with attaining objectives. As a result, it may be necessary to alter or completely revise an employee's objectives during the rating period. Like setting the initial objectives, this needs to be done collaboratively between managers and employees and requires ongoing communication to determine if additional changes are needed.

Prior to giving feedback to address a performance issue, it's important to diagnose why an employee may be experiencing that problem. This is important because what you do to address a problem will vary based on its underlying cause. As examples:

- Sometimes performance problems result from *unclear expectations*, which are generally easy to fix.
- If expectations are clear, an employee may *lack the skills* to perform and need training in relevant areas.
- Lack of *motivation* is another possible source of performance problems. A person could be de-motivated by things at work or home.

Best Practices and Realities:
Ongoing Feedback

Best Practice

- Provide regular, on-going feedback
- Give specific, actionable feedback in close proximity to the performance event

Realities

- Both managers and employees are uncomfortable with and avoid feedback conversations
- In many organizations, managers and employees differ in their perceptions about the presence of feedback
  - Managers perceive they provide extensive feedback to employees
  - Employees perceive they receive less feedback from their managers
- Need to evaluate the organization's culture for feedback – many do not support ongoing feedback processes and may require culture changes in this area
- Need to train managers and employees on their joint responsibilities in the feedback process
- Need job-relevant performance standards to facilitate delivering feedback

---

In these situations, it helpful to find out the nature of the problem, so it can be addressed in the most reasonable way possible.

- Another source of below standards performance is *environment or work process factors*. If the employee doesn't have the tools needed to perform work effectively, additional resources or other interventions may be necessary to address the issue.

The bottom line is that you need to first understand what's causing a performance problem before you can address it.

For feedback to have value, it needs to be given in close proximity to the event.[3] It does not help employees to receive feedback nine months after something has happened. And an employee's performance will not likely improve by itself while the manager waits for the end-of-year review to say something. Research has shown that in organizations where employees report higher levels of ongoing, informal feedback, performance levels are higher.

Tips:
Guidelines for Providing Feedback Effectively[4,5,6]
• Diagnose the reason for the performance issue • Provide immediate positive or developmental feedback in a private location • Ask for the employee's view about what could have been done differently • Be specific about what behaviors were effective or ineffective • Focus on what the person did or did not do, not personal characteristics • Collaboratively plan steps to address the issue • Offer help in addressing performance issues and providing resources

There is debate about whether the performance management cycle should include formal interim review sessions, for example, on a quarterly or bi-annual basis. The advantage of these is that they promote performance conversations in situations where they may not be occurring regularly. The disadvantage of these is that they present another requirement for already busy managers and employees to fulfill. If managers and employees are engaging in effective informal conversations, these should be occurring whenever something happens to prompt them. This is the ideal situation. If there is not a good climate for feedback, however, and informal conversations are not occurring to the extent they should be, it may be necessary to include formal interim review sessions in the performance management process.

For feedback to work well, it must be a two-way communication process and joint responsibility between managers and employees, not just the manager's responsibility.[7,8] In some organizations, there is a culture that encourages providing candid, regular feedback to achieve continuous improvement. However, more often than not, both managers and employees avoid feedback discussions – managers fear damaging relationships with employees and employees do not want to jeopardize access to rewards. Contributing to this problem is that many managers and employees are not comfortable talking about performance issues. Thus, an effective first step in addressing feedback issues is to formally assess an organization's culture for feedback and the extent to which managers and employees perceive that feedback is given and received. This not only provides information about organizational members' perceptions about the availability of feedback, but it also provides a gauge regarding their motivation to engage in performance conversations.

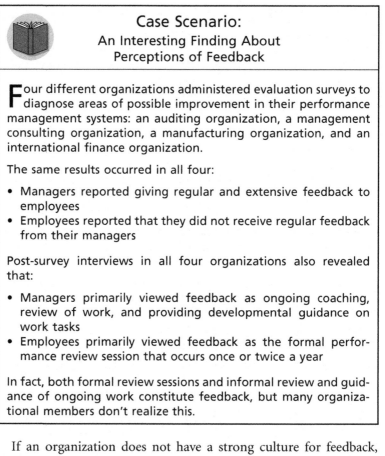

Case Scenario:
An Interesting Finding About Perceptions of Feedback

Four different organizations administered evaluation surveys to diagnose areas of possible improvement in their performance management systems: an auditing organization, a management consulting organization, a manufacturing organization, and an international finance organization.

The same results occurred in all four:

- Managers reported giving regular and extensive feedback to employees
- Employees reported that they did not receive regular feedback from their managers

Post-survey interviews in all four organizations also revealed that:

- Managers primarily viewed feedback as ongoing coaching, review of work, and providing developmental guidance on work tasks
- Employees primarily viewed feedback as the formal performance review session that occurs once or twice a year

In fact, both formal review sessions and informal review and guidance of ongoing work constitute feedback, but many organizational members don't realize this.

If an organization does not have a strong culture for feedback, steps can be taken to increase performance conversations between managers and employees as well as their understanding about what constitutes feedback. The reality is that both managers and employees benefit from training on their roles in the feedback process and engaging in ongoing feedback discussions throughout the rating cycle. The overall goal of training is to remove some of the formality and discomfort around giving and receiving feedback and to make this a more accepted, regular practice in the workplace.

Managers need training on how to provide feedback in a constructive, candid, and timely manner. Employees need training on how to seek feedback to ensure they understand how they are performing and how to react openly to the feedback they receive. In addition, assuming the performance management system contains defined performance standards, both managers and employees need training on how discuss employee performance in relation to the standards as part of the regular feedback process. Defined performance standards not only help make feedback more concrete, but they also avoid perceptions that managers are holding employees to idiosyncratic standards for which others are not accountable.

Tips:
What Managers and Employees Can Do to Increase Feedback

Manager Responsibilities
- Provide timely and actionable feedback – most important is ongoing and informal feedback given as part of the daily routine
- Provide guidance on specific tasks that help employees accomplish work
- Compliment behaviors when employees perform well
- Provide ongoing, informal feedback – managers and employees often do not recognize ongoing, informal feedback as feedback, but it is!

Employee Responsibilities
- Seek feedback if there is ambiguity or questions about performance or standing
- Manage own career and performance
- Do not rely on managers to provide sufficient feedback unprompted

---

An additional important aspect of feedback training is to teach managers how to handle different reactions to feedback that employees may have. Depending on the personality of employees, they may be more or less open to feedback and more or less willing to accept it. Feedback reactions can vary from positive and accepting to negative and angry. It is important for managers to recognize and effectively manage different reactions to feedback.

Example:
Performance Feedback from Manager

Assume that a manager gave the following feedback to an employee:

"I noticed during the meeting that you rolled your eyes each time John spoke up and offered his input. If others in your group see this, they might lose respect for you, which may make it difficult for you to get things done. You might want to try avoiding this behavior in the future."

Here are different ways an employee might react to this feedback and tips for handling these.

Tips:
How to Handle Different Reactions to Feedback

Acceptance

- The individual agrees with your feedback
  - "You're right. I noticed that myself about halfway through. Thanks for pointing it out."

Surprise or Shock

- The individual did not anticipate your feedback but generally accepts it
  - "I didn't realize I did that – I usually don't show my feelings."
- Strategy
  - Listen to what the individual has to say, recognize the surprise and move on
  - "Sometimes it's difficult to know when we do things like that – it's often subconscious."

Continued

Defensiveness

- The individual makes excuses for why the behavior was appropriate
  - "John generally provides input that's off-point. Plus, every time I said something, he got a scowl on his face."
- Strategy
  - Listen to what the individual has to say, reiterate what needs improvement and why, and don't argue or become defensive yourself
  - "I understand how that could be frustrating, but we were discussing *your* performance. If others see you roll your eyes, they might lose respect and that could impede your ability to get things done."

Anger
- The individual gets irritated with you
  - "I can't believe you're giving me this feedback. I'm certain I didn't do that."
- Strategy:
  - Listen to what the individual has to say, remind the individual of your role, and reiterate your feedback
  - "Part of my job is to give you feedback on things I see. In the meeting, I noticed you rolled your eyes each time John spoke up."

Rejection

- The individual does not agree with your feedback and does not accept it
  - "You must be mistaken. I work very hard to make sure I don't do things like that."
- Strategy:
  - Listen to what the individual has to say, validate the individual's perspective, and reiterate what you observed
  - "I know you do and understand that you may not realize what was happening. Sometimes things like this happen subconsciously but it's what I saw."

Beyond the training provided or the climate for feedback, a factor that affects feedback effectiveness is the interpersonal relationship between the manager and employee. If there is not a basic level of trust between the manager and employee, it is unlikely that their communication and feedback process will be productive or lead to positive results. Alternatively, when there is trust between managers and employees, both are more willing to open up and talk candidly about performance, which is essential for development and growth. Employees are also more willing to follow the lead of a manager they trust, because they believe they will be treated fairly. There are several behaviors that managers can engage in to increase trust with employees.

Tips:
How Managers Can Increase Trust

- *Make realistic commitments.* Be realistic about what you can do and communicate that. If you can't promise an outcome, make a realistic prediction of the likelihood of an outcome.
- *Explain changes in plans.* If you need to do something different than you've communicated, let people know what changed and how that affects things.
- *Close the loop.* Tell others you've done what you said you would do. Sometimes you do what you promised, but people don't know it.
- *Provide evidence of a win-win.* If you promote one's interests at the expense of another, even the person who comes out ahead will suspect your motives. Show that you're interested in everyone's benefit, and what you've done to be fair.
- *Protect the interests of people who aren't present.* If you share information with some and not others or criticize others, people will be less willing to trust you. By showing concern for people who aren't present, those who are present feel that you will treat them the same way when they're not around.
- *Show support.* Trying things out of one's comfort zone is part of development but can also make people apprehensive. Acknowledge people's apprehension while building their self-confidence. For example, "I know you're nervous about this, but I wouldn't ask you to do it if I didn't think you would do a good job."
- *Verify understanding.* Don't assume that people know what you're doing for them. Talk to them about their concerns and how your actions support them.
- *Show employees you can get things done.* Employees need to see that you have the skills, judgment, and influence to carry out your promises.

- *Admit your limits.* Employees trust managers more if you're honest and genuine with them than if you make promises you can't keep.
- *Showcase what you know.* Don't be boastful, but let people know about your experience, expertise, and qualifications. Stay current in your field and develop yourself as a coach.
- *Offer status reports and forecasts.* Tell employees what you do and don't know, and what you can and cannot tell them. If you don't know something, say that. If you can't discuss something, tell them when you can.
- *Communicate consistent principles.* Let employees know what principles guide your decisions and follow these as much as possible.
- *Explain your actions.* Your intentions are not always apparent, especially when the situation is complex. Explain changes or discrepancies in your actions, so employees know why you are doing something that may appear inconsistent.
- *Balance candor with discretion.* Before disclosing information, consider its good versus its harm. Would disclosure be a breach of confidence? Would it hurt the person's feelings without reason? When is the best time or place to share the information?

Practical Exercise

At the end of this chapter, practical Training Exercise 1 can be used to teach managers how to build trust.

Step 4. Employees Provide Input on Own Perceptions of Performance

Collecting employee input is a useful strategy to enhance ownership and acceptance of a performance management process. Understanding employees' perceptions of their own effectiveness also helps managers deal with them more effectively. Employees who significantly underestimate their capabilities need to be treated differently than those who overestimate their worth. In the former case, reinforcement and confidence building are warranted whereas in the latter case, confidence neutralizing is needed!

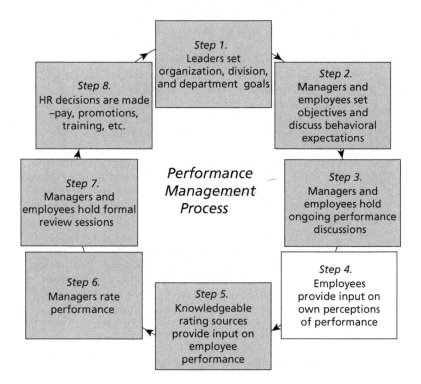

Best Practices and Realities:
Employee Input

Best Practice

• Employees rate themselves on rating scales

Realities

• Providing self-ratings on rating scales can cause unnecessary conflicts between managers and staff
• Preferable approach is to collect statements of most meritorious accomplishments or other narrative input
• Employees need training on how to write accomplishment statements

Providing employees an opportunity to provide input into the performance management process is considered a best practice and has been well received in many organizations. This often takes the form of asking employees to provide self-ratings on whatever rating scale is being used, which are then compared to the manager's ratings of the employee and discussed. Although this is a common practice, this approach can lead to unnecessary defensiveness, disagreements, and negative feelings between employees and managers, especially if managers rate employees less favorably than they rate themselves. One caveat is that if the purpose of the appraisal is strictly development, self-ratings can be instructive. They are also unlikely to result in long-term negative feelings, even if they produce some initial defensiveness or disagreement. However, when ratings are tied to important outcomes, self-ratings are much more risky. Even if employees know they are not the most effective performers, some feel they have no choice but to rate themselves at the highest levels, so they don't do anything to jeopardize their rewards. This can exacerbate differences in the ratings provided by employees and managers and lead to difficulties in resolving these differences.

An alternative and more effective way of collecting employee input is for employees to prepare statements describing their most meritorious accomplishments during the rating period. A very large number of organizations, including auditing organizations, information technology organizations, product sales organizations, consulting organizations, service organizations, financial institutions, and government agencies, have incorporated the use of accomplishments in their performance management systems.

Although the idea of writing accomplishments may seem straightforward and simple, the reality is that the quality of accomplishments produced by employees is highly variable. It is best to provide detailed instructions, if not actual training, on how to write accomplishment statements. Also, human resources departments sometimes offer to review and assist with drafting employee accomplishment statements to ensure that they clearly and accurately convey the employee's contributions. If the goal of the accomplishment statements is simply to provide employee input, well-composed accomplishment statements are helpful but not essential. However, if goal is to use the accomplishment statements in making pay, promotion, or other important decisions, providing training to ensure that effective statements are prepared becomes much more important.

Good to Know:
Advantages of Accomplishment Statements

- Makes employees active participants in the performance management process.
- Reminds managers about the results employees have delivered, and how these results were achieved.
- Provides insight regarding employees' views of their performance. A recommended practice is to have employees and managers collaborate on the wording of the accomplishments, as this helps to minimize disconnects between the manager's and employee's views of the employee's contributions.
- Provides content that can be integrated into the formal narrative comments that managers include in their appraisals, reducing the amount of writing the manager has to do.
- Provides documented performance information that can be retained over multiple years and used not only for immediate pay decisions but also for future promotion decisions or other human resources actions. Research has shown that employee accomplishments are effective predictors of how employees will perform at higher job levels.[9] Thus, they provide useful input for promotion decisions.

Tips:
Guidelines for Writing Employee Accomplishments

Situation or circumstances faced:
Describe the situation, circumstances, audience, or program that is the subject of your accomplishment. This is important to provide a context for understanding what you did to address the issues, problems, or circumstances you faced. If the circumstances involved difficult, complex, or stressful situations, be sure to clearly describe what made the situation particularly difficult, complex, or stressful.

Specific actions taken:
Describe the actions you took in sufficient detail that the reader can readily understand why and how your actions made a significant contribution. Describe what you did or said using specific

behaviors, and avoid using general statements to describe your actions. For example, in relating how you persuaded someone to a point of view, it would not be effective to say that you "used good arguments that were persuasive." Instead, discuss exactly what arguments you used, why these were good arguments to make, to whom you made them, and how the arguments ultimately succeeded in swaying another person to your viewpoint. If you were part of a team that made a major contribution, you need to describe *your specific* activities, role, and responsibilities on that team.

Impact the unit or organization:
Explain the results and impact of your actions. For example, if an accomplishment resulted in work being conducted more efficiently, describe the efficiencies that were realized and the time your actions saved in completing work. Be sure to discuss the significance and importance of the outcomes you achieved for your team, office, or the organization.

Evaluations of accomplishment statements have revealed several common problems. Instead of writing about a specific contribution or result, employees sometimes discuss general work behaviors that they regularly perform on the job. If they do write about a specific accomplishment, they may neglect to say exactly what they did to achieve the outcome. Another issue is that employees often do not know how to convey the impact of their accomplishments. And, finally, employees sometimes discuss what a group achieved rather than what they did as an individual contributor. So the bottom line is that accomplishment statements can be a very useful and effective way to collect employee input but it takes training and a commitment of time and effort to produce good accomplishment statements.

Example:
Employee Accomplishment Statement

Situation: Responsible for planning and organizing a major meeting aimed at demonstrating the new automated performance management system that was being implemented organization-wide, including identifying a location for the meeting that

Continued

would accommodate 1200 expected attendees, planning the agenda, and coordinating with three vendors that had different responsibilities for system development and implementation. This was a very important conference with potentially significant impact, because the conference was geared to showcasing the new system to users.

Action: Independently arranged for all details (space, materials, audiovisual requirements, refreshments, parking) and ensured the program and materials were finalized one month in advance. Made arrangements to have materials copied and packaged two weeks in advance of the conference, so that there would be time to deal with any problems that might occur. Contacted and confirmed attendance with all organizational representatives one month before the conference and again two weeks before the conference. Developed contingency plans for anything that might go wrong (e.g., participants cancelling at last minute, equipment not working). The day of the conference, the audio visual equipment provided by the facility did not work. Because of the contingency plan I had prepared which involved having back-up equipment available, the conference proceeded as planned without delay.

Result: As a result of my thorough planning, the meeting ran smoothly, no major problems occurred, and users were sufficiently impressed that they reported motivation to use and positive regard for the new system.

Timeframe: August–October 2008

Supervisor to Verify: Mary Smith (678) 346-9978

Practical Exercise

At the end of this chapter, practical Training Exercise 2 can be used to teach employees how to write effective accomplishment statements.

Step 5. Knowledgeable Rating Sources Provide Input on Employee Performance

Obtaining performance information from managers, peers, direct reports, and customers is often referred to as 360-degree feedback.

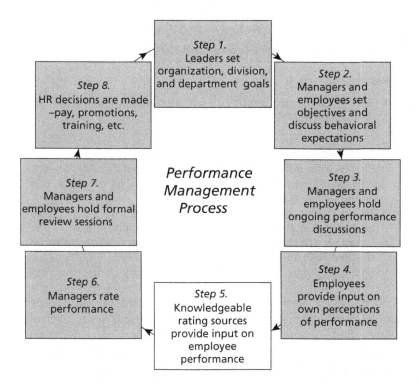

Numerous books and articles have been written about this topic, for example:

- Ghorpade, J. (2000). Managing the five paradoxes of 360-degree feedback. *Academy of Management Executive, 14*(1), 140–150.
- Waldman, D., & Atwater, L. E. (1998). *The power of 360-degree feedback: How to leverage performance evaluations for top productivity.* Houston, TX: Gulf Publishing.

One advantage of using rating sources other than the manager is that they often view different aspects of an employee's performance and collectively provide a more complete picture of a person's effectiveness. For example, managers would not typically have full information or the necessary perspective to evaluate how effectively an employee develops or leads her subordinates, whereas direct reports would be an excellent source for this information.

Best Practices and Realities:
Multi-Source Ratings

Best Practice

- Gain input from others with first-hand knowledge of performance

Realities

- Ratings from other sources should not be used directly for decision-making; the manager should serve as gate-keeper and provide final evaluation
- Rating quality decreases when multi-source ratings are used for decision-making versus strictly development
- To obtain effective development, multi-source ratings must be coupled with targeted development programs

---

Collecting performance information from multiple rating sources can be done informally or formally. If done formally, this involves a fairly complex administrative process. First, with the exception of the manager, ratings should be collected from *at least* three feedback providers from each rating source (e.g., three direct reports, three customers, etc.). In order to protect the anonymity of individual raters and provide a safe environment for providing feedback, ratings need to be averaged across the feedback providers from a given source (e.g., all peer ratings are averaged) before reporting them to the employee. Employees are usually provided with comprehensive feedback reports, showing the average score on each item by rater group – that is, average rating score from peer group, the average rating score from direct report group, the average score from customer group, and so forth. Narrative comments are also provided to the employee. Automated processes to collect, analyze, and integrate formal ratings from multiple sources are best because they help to make this somewhat complex data collection process efficient and manageable.

In most situations, multi-source feedback programs are used strictly to provide development feedback. Research has shown that to obtain the maximum benefit and highest degree of performance improvement from these programs, they must be coupled with targeted development programs that specifically address identified per-

Good to Know: Two Ways to Collect Multi-Source Feedback	
Informal	Formal
• Manager reaches out to others with whom the individual has worked • Manager gathers perceptions from feedback providers and considers these when making his or her ratings • Information is usually collected in verbal conversations or informal written documents prepared strictly for the manager's consideration • Manager decides what weight to put on different sources' feedback and what information to consider in his or her ratings	• Standardized rating form is sent to requested feedback providers • Raters complete the form, typically providing ratings of the frequency with which they have observed certain behaviors and also providing narrative comments • Ratings are automatically collected and analyzed by rating source, for example, all peer ratings are averaged • Reports are prepared summarizing the ratings and narratives provided by rating source • If used for decision-making, ratings are automatically combined into final ratings

formance gaps. When used for development, it is not necessary to exercise as much control over the information sources and data collection process as when the information is used for decision-making. There is also no need to combine the average ratings from the different sources into one overall numerical score, because the purpose of the assessment is to inform on development planning. Alternatively, if performance ratings are used for decision-making, managers should serve as gate-keepers for integrating the information obtained from different rating sources, judging its credibility and quality, and balancing it against other available information. The reason why control and proper integration of information is especially important for decision-making purposes is because direct reports, peers, and customers often do not have the qualifications, experience, complete perspective, or motivation to make accurate and effective ratings.

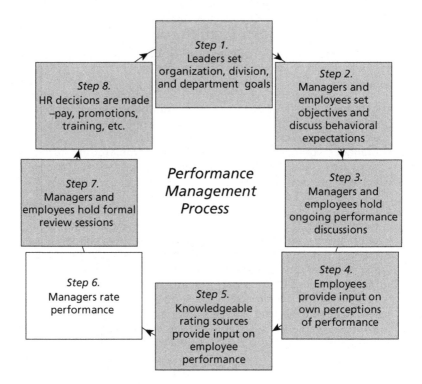

Step 1.
Leaders set organization, division, and department goals

Step 2.
Managers and employees set objectives and discuss behavioral expectations

Step 8.
HR decisions are made –pay, promotions, training, etc.

Performance Management Process

Step 3.
Managers and employees hold ongoing performance discussions

Step 7.
Managers and employees hold formal review sessions

Step 4.
Employees provide input on own perceptions of performance

Step 6.
Managers rate performance

Step 5.
Knowledgeable rating sources provide input on employee performance

Step 6. Managers Rate Performance

As discussed, best practice in performance management is to consider both job behavior and results using defined performance standards as a basis for making ratings.

Performance standards help employees understand what is expected of them and provide common standards for managers to use in evaluating employees, thereby increasing consistency, transparency, and fairness. Perceptions of fairness are important and can avoid negative outcomes that might otherwise result from unfavorable ratings, such as employees challenging their evaluations.[10] Thus, the inclusion of performance standards to guide ratings is essential for an effective performance management system.[11]

An example Rating Form is shown in Figure 4.4, including performance standards for evaluating both results and behaviors. It contains objectives to be achieved, rating standards, performance narrative, areas to be developed and development actions, and signature blocks for the manager and employee.

Rating Form

Employee's Name _____   Manager's Name _____

Objectives to be Achieved:
1.
2.
3.
4.
5.

Results Assessment

Objective 1: _____

1	2	3	4	5
Below Expectations Did not meet timeliness, quality, quantity, or impact goals.		Meets Expectations Met timeliness, quality, quantity, and financial metrics.		Exceeds Expectations Exceeded timeliness, quality, quantity, and financial goals.

1	2	3	4	5
Low Impact Result was straightforward to accomplish and had a small impact on business results.		Moderate Impact Result had a positive and discernable impact on efficiency or effectiveness of operations.		High Impact Result had an extremely positive impact, producing significant cost reductions or profit increases.

Objective 2: _____

1	2	3	4	5
Below Expectations Did not meet timeliness, quality, quantity, or financial metrics.		Meets Expectations Met timeliness, quality, quantity, and financial metrics.		Exceeds Expectations Exceeded timeliness, quality, quantity, and financial goals.

1	2	3	4	5
Low Impact Result was straightforward to accomplish and had a small impact on business results.		Moderate Impact Result had a positive and discernable impact on efficiency or effectiveness of operations.		High Impact Result had an extremely positive impact, producing significant cost reductions or profit increases.

Behavioral Assessment of Competencies

Planning Work

1	2	3	4	5
Below Expectations Fails to prioritize work for self or others to ensure timely completion of projects and assignments. Does not anticipate or take steps to mitigate obstacles that impact work schedule or delivery.		Meets Expectations Independently prioritizes, plans, organizes, and schedules own work activities to ensure assignments are completed in a timely manner. Coordinates work activities with coworkers and work unit; takes initiative to keep others informed of progress, problems, or changes. Sees obvious problems and makes recommendations to overcome them so that progress is not impeded.		**Exceeds Expectations** **"Meets Expectations" plus does the following:** Demonstrates exceptional skill in complex planning across organizational units and solving thorny logistical problems, resulting in contributions far beyond what is expected at this level. Takes initiative to help others plan efforts for the group to ensure goals are met. Anticipates important roadblocks and takes effective preemptive action to prevent them, ensuring effective progress on projects.

Figure 4.4 Rating form

Communication

1	2	3	4	5

Below Expectations	Meets Expectations	Exceeds Expectations
<standards appear here>	<standards appear here>	<standards appear here>

Collaborating with Others

1	2	3	4	5

Below Expectations	Meets Expectations	Exceeds Expectations
<standards appear here>	<standards appear here>	<standards appear here>

Representing the Organization

1	2	3	4	5

Below Expectations	Meets Expectations	Exceeds Expectations
<standards appear here>	<standards appear here>	<standards appear here>

Critical Thinking

1	2	3	4	5

Below Expectations	Meets Expectations	Exceeds Expectations
<standards appear here>	<standards appear here>	<standards appear here>

Technical Proficiency

1	2	3	4	5

Below Expectations	Meets Expectations	Exceeds Expectations
<standards appear here>	<standards appear here>	<standards appear here>

Learning and Developing

1	2	3	4	5

Below Expectations	Meets Expectations	Exceeds Expectations
<standards appear here>	<standards appear here>	<standards appear here>

Strategic Thinking

1	2	3	4	5

Below Expectations	Meets Expectations	Exceeds Expectations
<standards appear here>	<standards appear here>	<standards appear here>

Key Accomplishments: (completed by employee)

Accomplishment 1 **Situation:**

Action:

Result:

Timeframe   Verification

Accomplishment 2 **Situation:**

Action:

Result:

Timeframe   Verification

Narrative Comments (completed by manager):

Areas to be Developed:	Actions	Completion Date

Manager's Signature:_____ Date:_____

Employee's Signature:_____ Date:_____

The employee signature indicates receipt of, but not necessarily concurrence with, the evaluation herein.

Figure 4.4 *Continued*

Best Practices and Realities:
Performance Evaluation

Best Practice

- Evaluate job behaviors and results
- Make ratings against defined rating standards to facilitate consistency, fairness, and accuracy
- Provide narrative comments to further describe the rationale for ratings and promote more meaningful and conscientious feedback from managers

Realities

- Even with defined rating standards, managers frequently make common rating errors
- There are significant forces operating in organizations that yield lenient ratings
- Obtaining accurate ratings from managers that effectively distinguish between more and less effective performers requires training, monitoring, and incentives
- Managers often write poor narratives and require training and feedback to do this well

Good to Know:
Advantages of Performance Standards

- Communicate key performance factors and expectations
- Show distinctions in effectiveness levels that help supervisors explain why an employee was evaluated in a particular way
- Provide a job-relevant basis for evaluating employees, increasing fairness

To make performance ratings, managers review the employee accomplishments, the information obtained from knowledgeable rating sources (e.g., peers, customers), and the performance standards for the employee's job and level. The manager then compares the employee's performance to the pre-defined rating standards. The standards are not intended to be used as a checklist. Rather, managers need to select a rating for each performance area that best describes the employee's *typical* performance throughout the rating period. Definitions for the five-point rating scales that appear on the Rating Form are shown below.

Example:
Definition of Rating Scale Points

5 = Almost always performs as described by the "Exceeds Expectations" standards

4 = Sometimes performs as described by the "Exceeds Expectations" standards and sometimes performs as described by the "Meets Expectations" standards

3 = Almost always performs as described by the "Meets Expectations" standards

2 = Sometimes performs as described by the "Meets Expectations" standards and sometimes performs as described by the "Below Expectations" standards

1 = Almost always performs as described by the "Below Expectations" standards

---

Common Rating Errors Managers Make When Evaluating Performance

When evaluating employee performance, managers often make several common rating errors. Learning about these errors can help raters avoid them. The first rating error is Halo Error. It occurs when a manager's overall impression of an employee influences all of the manager's ratings. For example, if a manager feels an employee is a good performer overall, this overall impression will cause the manager to rate that employee high in all of the rating categories. To avoid this error, it's important to keep in mind that most employees do not perform at exactly the same level in all of the performance rating areas. Everyone has strengths and development areas, and the ratings should reflect these.

Single Time Error occurs when ratings fail to reflect typical performance and instead are based on only one or a few performance instances. An employee might do one thing really well or really poorly, leading the manager to give a higher or lower rating than he otherwise might have given without this one instance of performance. It is important that ratings reflect the employee's typical performance throughout the rating period and not be overly influenced by a single performance event. An exception to this general rule could occur if an employee did something on the job that had such extremely serious negative consequences that it did, in fact, override all other instances of more effective performance.

The next error is Stereotype Error, which occurs when raters let stereotypes influence their ratings. For example, an employee's age, education, or gender may predispose managers to think they will perform well in some areas and less well in others. It is important not to let preconceived notions or stereotypes influence perceptions about an employee's capabilities or potential to perform a job. Managers need to keep an open mind, and be even-handed in the opportunities they provide staff. Managers also need to base their ratings on observed performance rather than their impressions about a person's strengths and weaknesses that are based on personal characteristics.

The last error is called Leniency/Severity Error. This is a tendency for some managers to rate all of their employees on the high side – if they are lenient raters – or the low side – if they are severe raters, irrespective of how employees actually perform. Managers can overcome leniency or severity by comparing employee performance to the rating standards. If a five-point rating scale is used properly, the most common rating should be a 3, assuming that this scale point means an employee is fully meeting the expectations for the job. That said, many managers suffer from leniency problems, which are discussed in detail next.

Addressing Rating Leniency

Although managers can make various rating errors when they evaluate performance, the most important thing is that managers rate each employee accurately. Accurate ratings that clearly distinguish between more and less effective performers provide valuable information to

Tips:
Summary of How to Avoid Common Rating Errors

Halo Error

- Manager's overall impression of an employee influences all of the ratings
  - "Jose's a good worker; I'll give him 4s across the board."
- To avoid error
  - Remember, all employees have strengths and development areas
  - Consider the employee's performance separately for each rating dimension or competency

Single Time Error

- Manager bases ratings on one or two performance incidents
  - "Maria stayed late for two weeks straight to help the team complete an important report by the due date; I'll give her a 5 for Teamwork."
- To avoid error
  - Ratings should reflect typical performance throughout the rating period. It's helpful to keep notes reflecting incidents of especially effective and ineffective performance throughout the evaluation period.

Stereotype Error

- Manager allows personal or demographic factors to influence ratings
  - "Leah's young, so she does not have the maturity or expertise to provide advice to clients that is of great value; she can't be more than a 3 on Client Orientation."
- To avoid error
  - Be aware that stereotypes can affect your ratings
  - Make ratings in relation to actual observed performance

Leniency/Severity Error

- Rater consistently assigns ratings that are too high or too low
  - "We've had a great year – everyone deserves ratings of 4 or 5."
- To avoid error
  - Use the performance standards as a basis for making your ratings

employees and are necessary to make fair decisions regarding pay, promotions, assignments, and other actions. Unfortunately, there are many forces operating in organizations that lead managers to provide lenient ratings. Furthermore, ratings from most performance management systems tend to grow increasingly lenient over time, until they become almost useless for decision-making or development. This occurs for various reasons including: (1) increasing pressure on managers from employees over time to provide higher ratings, (2) managers not wanting to harm their direct reports in terms of access to rewards, especially if other managers are providing lenient ratings, and (3) actual performance improvements as employees work towards achieving the evaluation standards.

Before discussing what can be done to deal with lenient ratings, it is important to understand when leniency reflects a problem with the ratings and when leniency reflects reality. In most organizations, if no rating errors were committed by managers, the average performance rating would likely be above the mid-point of the scale. This is because most people want to do well on their jobs and try to perform as effectively as they can. As a result, most employees meet expectations and some exceed the expectations for their jobs. Likewise, employees who are consistently performing below expectations or not meeting expectations are counseled out of their jobs or provided training to address performance deficiencies. Therefore, if we look at the actual performance levels in most organizations, what we find is that ratings are at least somewhat skewed towards the high end of the scale.

Another factor that can result in higher ratings is if performance is being managed using performance standards. Under these circumstances, employees should be achieving results and adapting their behavior to align with the standards. Successful performance management would be expected to yield some increases in the ratings over time, reflecting the fact that the system is working to drive increasingly effective performance. Although somewhat higher ratings should be expected for these reasons, many organizations suffer very significant problems with leniency, where the ratings are so extremely positive that they probably are not realistic reflections of true performance levels.

In some organizations, the problem of lenient ratings is so pervasive that many experts advise implementation of new performance

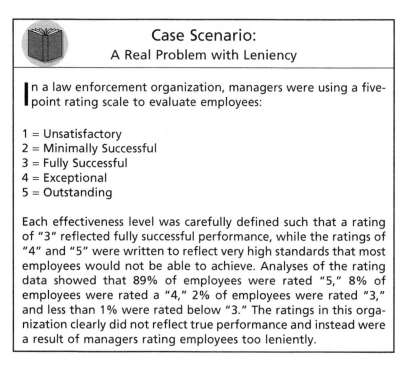

Case Scenario:
A Real Problem with Leniency

In a law enforcement organization, managers were using a five-point rating scale to evaluate employees:

1 = Unsatisfactory
2 = Minimally Successful
3 = Fully Successful
4 = Exceptional
5 = Outstanding

Each effectiveness level was carefully defined such that a rating of "3" reflected fully successful performance, while the ratings of "4" and "5" were written to reflect very high standards that most employees would not be able to achieve. Analyses of the rating data showed that 89% of employees were rated "5," 8% of employees were rated a "4," 2% of employees were rated "3," and less than 1% were rated below "3." The ratings in this organization clearly did not reflect true performance and instead were a result of managers rating employees too leniently.

management systems every few years, simply to start over and attempt to achieve more differentiated ratings of employees. This strategy generally works, until the new system quickly suffers the same leniency problems as the previous system. Thus, not only is it ineffective in the long run to implement a new performance management system every couple of years to mitigate leniency, but this is also disruptive and expensive. The problem is that implementation of a new system does not address either of the two major issues that underlie leniency:

- The first issue is that many managers do not want to disadvantage their employees in terms of the rewards they receive by rating them lower than other managers are rating their employees.
- The second issue is that there is a strong desire among employees to be rated as exceeding rather than simply meeting their job expectations.

Many employees view ratings that "meet expectations" as a negative message that indicates they are not performing well. Not wanting to de-motivate or upset employees in most circumstances, managers feel pressured to give ratings at the higher end of the scale. There are three strategies that have been used with variable success to address leniency issues in organizations.

Develop a new system

- As discussed, changing the performance management system every few years to introduce a new rating scale and recalibrate ratings downward has not proven to be effective in the long run.

Force managers to rate to a predefined rating distribution

- This entails predetermining how many employees can receive ratings at each level. For example, only 10% can receive ratings of "5," only 20% can receive ratings of "4," 40% can receive ratings of "3," and so forth. This strategy is not recommended, however, especially when managers are rating small numbers of employees. This is because one manager's group may actually contain a higher proportion of high performing employees than another manager's group. By forcing the same proportion of ratings at each rating level within each group, true differences in performance between groups are not recognized. This can result in inaccurate conclusions about different employees' contributions and unfair distribution of rewards.

Standardize the ratings within groups

- This strategy allows the manager to rate however many people he or she wants at each rating level. However, a statistical procedure is performed that does not consider the rating level assigned to each employee but instead calculates how far each employee is rated from the average rating given by the manager to all of her employees. An assumption in using this method is that individuals who are more differentiated from other employees are actually performing much more or less effectively than those who are rated more closely together, irrespective of their absolute rating level. The overall goal of this strategy is to remove differences in the ratings that result from some managers rating more leniently (or severely) than others. As an example, assume one manager provided ratings of his employees where the average rating across all individuals was 4.5 (on a 5-point scale), and all employees were rated as either a 4 or a 5. Assume another manager provided ratings of her employees where the average rating was 3.0, but employees were rated using the entire scale. That is, ratings were given from 1–5. If the actual ratings were considered, most everyone in the first group might be given a higher raise than most everyone in the second group, because all of the employees in the first group received ratings of 4 or 5, whereas only a few employees in the second group received ratings of 4 or 5. What standardization does, essentially, is ignore the actual ratings but retains how far employees were rated from the average rating in their own group. For the manager who used only two of the rating scale points (e.g., 4 or 5), the standardized ratings for these employees would all be fairly close to the average rating of 4.5 that resulted for the group. Alternatively, for the manager who evaluated employees from 1–5 with an average rating of 3.0, some ratings (e.g., 2s and 4s) would be closer to the average rating of 3.0 than ratings of 1 or 5. The result is that those who were given a rating of 5 from the manager who used more rating points will receive a score that is further away from the average than those who were given a rating of 5 from the manager who used only ratings of 4 or 5. The way this information is typically interpreted is that employees who are rated further from the average of their work group are likely to be more extremely good or extremely poor performers and should be rewarded accordingly. Like the previous approach where managers are forced to rate to a predetermined distribution, this strategy makes the assumption that the average performance in different groups of employees is truly equivalent, which may not be the case.

Training and monitoring
- The final strategy for addressing leniency issues is to implement training, communications, and monitoring programs to promote accurate ratings. One component of this approach is to change the culture and expectations around ratings such that "Meets Expectations" is viewed as a desirable evaluation for employees who are effectively fulfilling their job requirements. Accordingly, this should be the expected rating as well as the rating received by

most employees. A second component of this strategy is to monitor, provide feedback, and evaluate managers on the extent to which they provide accurate ratings, identify employee strengths and development areas, and distinguish between effective and less effective performers. The training and monitoring strategy, if successful, is the most effective approach for dealing with rating leniency issues because it does not impose assumptions about the performance of employees across groups like the forced distribution and standardization strategies discussed above. Training and monitoring approaches focus on changing an organization's culture around the meaning of ratings, recalibrating thinking around what ratings to expect, and reinforcing managers to make accurate distinctions between employees. Accordingly, this is the most effective long-term strategy to implement. That said, this is also a difficult strategy to implement successfully, especially in larger, more dispersed organizations.

Narratives to Support Ratings

In most performance management systems, the rating process allows for, if not requires, narratives to be written to support the ratings. In many organizations, however, managers are overworked and have numerous responsibilities beyond managing people. Additionally, most managers have multiple direct reports and most performance management systems cover at least six months to a year, meaning there is a large amount of performance information that is difficult, if not impossible, to recall accurately. These factors can contribute to managers basing their appraisals on general impressions of employees developed over time, which may be accurate or may be fraught with bias. Irrespective of how accurate these developed impressions are, providing feedback to employees based on impressions rather than actual performance causes difficulties when managers need to explain exactly what the employee did that deserved a particular rating. The requirement to provide narrative comments has the benefit of motivating managers to take steps to recall concrete performance examples, which facilitates both rating accuracy and having more meaningful feedback discussions.

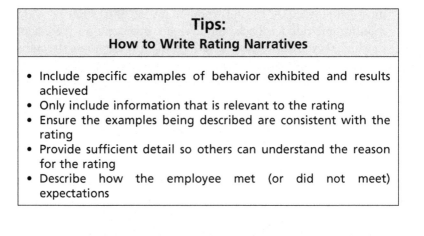

Tips:
How to Write Rating Narratives

- Include specific examples of behavior exhibited and results achieved
- Only include information that is relevant to the rating
- Ensure the examples being described are consistent with the rating
- Provide sufficient detail so others can understand the reason for the rating
- Describe how the employee met (or did not meet) expectations

On the surface, writing a performance narrative may seem simple. However, all the guidance that applies to providing verbal feedback also applies to writing narratives. For example, it is important to be specific, ensure that the feedback is actionable, focus on behavior or results rather than personal characteristics. A challenge is that narratives often do not support the ratings that were given. In fact, in evaluation studies where managers were asked what ratings they thought had been given based on another manager's narrative, many instances of misalignment were found. Narratives that do not clearly and obviously support the numerical ratings can cause serious problems, especially if the performance management system is legally challenged. It is therefore important that managers' narrative comments provide clear descriptions of performance that support the ratings. Strategies to facilitate this include training managers how to prepare effective narratives and having the narratives reviewed by human resources or higher-level managers. Shown below are excerpts that suffer from common difficulties associated with narratives – being too general, non-behavioral, and personal – and how these could be improved.

	Example: How to Improve Rating Narratives	
Competency	**Poor Narrative**	**Improved Narrative**
Collaborating with Others	Poor interpersonal skills with others	Did not provide supervisor with updates on project status despite repeated requests
Communicating with Others	Excellent writer	Rewrote technical report to clearly and understandably present complex information to a non-technical audience
Technical Proficiency	Poor technical knowledge	On three occasions, provided customers with incorrect information on procedures

Practical Exercise

At the end of this chapter, practical Training Exercise 3 can be used to teach managers how to write effective narrative statements.

Step 7. Managers and Employees Hold Formal Review Sessions

Assuming feedback has been provided on a regular basis, the formal performance review session should be a recap of what occurred throughout the rating period. In other words, there should be no new information, especially about performance deficiencies that is brought up for the first time in the formal review session. Any issues of this nature should have been addressed in a timely manner when they occurred. Prior to the formal review, both managers and employees should spend time planning what they want to cover. While one part of the review should focus on the ratings and narrative comments,[12]

Step 1.
Leaders set organization, division, and department goals

Step 2.
Managers and employees set objectives and discuss behavioral expectations

Step 8.
HR decisions are made –pay, promotions, training, etc.

Performance Management Process

Step 3.
Managers and employees hold ongoing performance discussions

Step 7.
Managers and employees hold formal review sessions

Step 4.
Employees provide input on own perceptions of performance

Step 6.
Managers rate performance

Step 5.
Knowledgeable rating sources provide input on employee performance

Best Practices and Realities:
Performance Review

Best Practice

- Should be a recap – not a first notice of performance issues
- Should be forward-looking and developmentally focused

Reality

- Need to train managers and employees about their roles and **responsibilities** in conducting effective review sessions
- Diagnosing development needs is much easier than addressing them
- Providing developmental suggestions targeted to each competency helps considerably

the majority of the session should be forward-looking and developmentally focused.

Experienced practitioners have found that performance standards help to identify and address development needs. Obviously, any rating area where the employee is not meeting expectations is an area for development. If the employee is fully meeting the expectations for the job, the discussion can focus on the employee's career aspirations and development activities that will help prepare her for advancement. One caveat about development planning is that managers need to be realistic about the competencies employees can likely develop and those that they are unlikely to develop. For example, most employees can develop enhanced technical knowledge and skills relevant to their jobs. However, innate abilities, like critical thinking or initiative, are less likely to be substantially improved through development efforts. Good managers assess and correctly diagnose the innate abilities of their direct reports. Rather than focus on improving performance in areas where this is unlikely, these managers play to their employees' strengths. They get the most from their staff by making assignments that capitalize on individual's abilities rather than repeatedly putting them in situations where they are unlikely to succeed. While recognition and assignments based on strengths are more effective strategies than trying to improve certain innate competencies that are difficult to develop, managers should nonetheless be prepared to address any low ratings with their direct reports and provide actionable feedback in response to employees' inquiries about what they can do to enhance their performance, even if significant strides are unlikely.

Another thing to remember is that development is more likely to be desired and achieved by younger employees who have less experience on a job. For these individuals, development tends to be as much about gaining experience doing higher-level work as it is about developing new competencies. As an example, an employee may desire to independently lead a complex technical project if his past experience has included leading only straightforward projects. Irrespective of whether the focus of development is acquiring technical knowledge, honing more innate competencies, or gaining experience, it is important to take into account the employee's motivation and desire for development. Like performance objectives, if employees aren't committed to achieving development objectives, managers cannot force progress in this area.

In some organizations, pay, promotion decisions, and other administrative actions are discussed during the formal performance review. In others, separate meetings are held to discuss administrative actions. The rationale for not discussing rewards or other outcomes during the formal performance review is to enable more open discussion about employee development. As a practical matter, however, it can be difficult to schedule multiple performance management meetings between managers and employees to discuss different aspects of the process – evaluations, development, and rewards. Likewise, if ratings are tied to rewards, separating the developmental discussion from the rewards discussion does not always lead to more open development discussions. This is because the parties know that rewards decisions will ultimately be made. Shown below is a suggested step-by-step process for conducting formal review sessions.

Tips:
Steps for Conducting the Formal Review Session

Step 1: Prepare for the Session

- Employees and managers must prepare to discuss
  - Key strengths and achievements
  - Development areas
  - Career options, given the person's skills and interests
  - How the manager can help

Step 2: Put Employee at Ease

- Meet in a private location
- Avoid interruptions

Step 3: Discuss the Purpose of the Session

- Outline the topics to be discussed in the session
- The review session is
  - a chance to learn about and try to resolve any problems
  - a chance to provide job performance feedback and coaching
- The review session is not
  - a first notice of poor performance – ineffective behavior should have been dealt with when it occurred
  - a time for disciplinary action

Step 4: Ask for the Employee's View

- What are your perceptions of your performance?
- How do you feel things are going on the job?
- What's going well and what problems are you experiencing?
- Is there anything that can be done to make the job easier to do?
- How do you feel about the job in general?

Step 5: Provide Recognition and Appreciation for Effective Performance

- Describe what the employee did that deserves recognition and why
- Discuss high ratings
- Discuss the value of the person's accomplishments to the work unit and organization
- Reinforce improvements from previous discussions

Step 6: Review Development Areas

- Clarify any areas where the employee feels improvement is needed
- Listen and respond to employee comments about development needs
- Review any low ratings and reasons for these in light of the performance standards
  - Employees should be aware of these before the session
- Focus on behaviors rather than personality traits
- Both employees and managers should contribute to discussion

Step 7: Review Steps to Improve Performance, if Needed

- Ask for the employee's input
- Offer suggestions and make commitments to help
- Come to agreement on future steps and expectations

Step 8: Discuss Employee's Career

- Ask the employee about career objectives and talk about these
- Provide realistic feedback the employee's longer-term potential
- Discuss specific steps for achieving goals (e.g., job assignments, on-the-job experiences, training)
- Commit to providing specific developmental experiences, if appropriate
- Create a timeline for accomplishing development steps

Continued

Step 9: Set Objectives for Upcoming Year

- Discuss any changes in the performance standards from the current rating period
- Discuss 3–5 key outcomes to be achieved
- Engage in a collaborative discussion

While identifying development needs can be fairly straightforward, knowing the best way to address these is not as easy. One of the first things many managers suggest to address any development need is formal training. Even in situations where formal training may be the best way to develop a skill, oftentimes neither managers nor employees know which specific training program will be best suited to a person's specific needs.

Good to Know:
The Relative Value of Formal Training

Formal training can be a useful way to gain job skills. However, formal training is expensive and what many people don't realize is that the vast majority of use-ful learning occurs on-the-job through relevant experience and not formal training.

To assist with development planning, some organizations provide a development resource as part of the performance management toolkit. These contain a variety of developmental experiences targeted to each performance area or competency that include on-the-job learning, formal training, and other development resources (e.g., books, web-sites). Once a development need is identified, a manager or employee can simply look up options for addressing that need. Development resources are particularly valuable if they are made available on-line where they can be easily searched.

While development resources have been well received by users, one caveat is that the information on training programs and internet sites needs to be regularly updated. Thus, there are maintenance requirements to be planned for and budgeted, if the resource is to remain up-to-date and useful. One strategy for reducing the maintenance costs of these resources is to exclude the training programs and inter-

Example:
Development Resource for
"Planning Work" Competency

Planning Work	Efficiently formulates and implements plans to accomplish goals, while keeping others informed on progress toward goals.
What does it involve?	• Adapts priorities according to the situational demands.
	• Formulates plans consistent with resources.
	• Adjusts plans to accommodate changing conditions or goals.
Key Questions	*To strengthen your organizing, planning, and coordinating skills, ask yourself the following questions every day:*

- Do I clarify what I am supposed to do before making a plan?
- Do I set realistic, yet ambitious deadlines?
- What could go wrong with this plan?
- Do I have contingency plans?
- What are the resources needed for this project?
- Have I coordinated this effort with the appropriate people?

Recommended Readings

- *Planning, Development, and Implementation.* Melcher, Bonita, & Kerzner, Harold (1988). Blue Ridge Summit, PA: TAB Books. HD30.28.M437.
- *Planning that Makes Things Happen: Getting From Where You Are to Where You Want to Be.* Bean, William C. (1993). Amherst, MA: Human Resource Development Press. HD30.28.B42.
- *Taking Charge: A Personal Guide to Managing Projects and Priorities.* Feder, Michael E. (1989). Mission, KS: Skillpath. HD30.28.F10.

Recommended Training Programs

- *Basic Project Management: Planning, Scheduling, and Control.* American Management Association. P.O. Box 319, Saranac Lake, NY 12983. (518) 891-0065.

Continued

- *How to Run a Small Project* (Self-Study). Graduate School, USDA. 1400 Wilson Boulevard, Suite 1000, Arlington, VA 22209-2312. (888) 744-4723.
- *Strategy Implementation: How to Get Your Plan Off the Shelf and into Action.* American Management Association. P.O. Box 319, Saranac Lake, NY 12983. (518) 891-0065.

On-the-Job Learning Activities

- Use project planning software (e.g., Microsoft Project).
- Shadow an employee/manager with extensive planning responsibilities who is good at organizing and planning. Take note of the techniques he or she uses and think about how you can apply these techniques to your planning activities.
- Plan a team meeting. Get feedback from your team members and team leader on your organizing and planning skills.
- Identify project managers with good planning and organization skills. Interview them about effective planning techniques. Apply one or more successful techniques to your projects.
- Review previous planning, organizing or coordinating activities for mistakes made and lessons learned.
- Volunteer to work on developing business or strategic plans. Get feedback on your planning skills from the people involved in this effort.
- Volunteer to coordinate a conference. Seek feedback from peers and managers on your effectiveness in this role.
- Co-lead a project. Solicit feedback from your team members and team leader on the project timeline and prioritization of activities.

net sites and only include on-the-job learning experiences and recommended readings, since these are more stable over time. Given that most learning occurs on the job, relevant job experience tends to be the most useful and cost-effective way to address many development needs.

Practical Exercise

At the end of this chapter, practical Training Exercise 4 can be used to teach managers and employees how to conduct an effective performance review session.

Step 8. HR Decisions are Made – Pay, Promotion, Termination

Increasingly, organizations are moving more towards linking performance management with important human resources outcomes. One of the most common performance-reward linkages is linking pay to performance, so the majority of our discussion will focus on that. However, performance management results are also sometimes used to inform on other important outcomes such as promotion and terminations. In the case of promotion decisions, performance appraisals are rarely the only measure that is used. Typically, there is consideration beyond current performance of whether candidates have the skills to perform successfully at the next level. Thus, effective performance in a current job is often treated as a necessary but not sufficient condition for promotion, and additional assessments are used that specifically focus on predicting success at the next level.

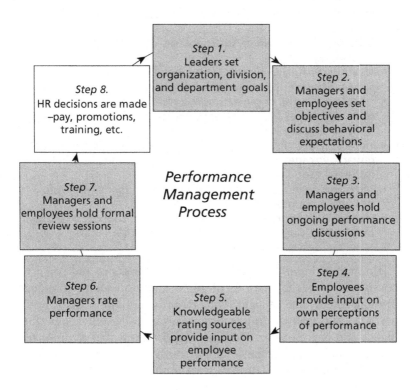

Likewise, for termination decisions, performance management results can certainly be used to identify and provide support for level or pay reductions or removal of employees. However, most organizations have additional processes (opportunity periods; formal performance improvement plans) that are more direct precursors to these actions.

Best Practices and Realities:
Tying Performance to HR Decisions

Best Practice

- Link performance to human resources outcomes
- Motivate performance and results through meaningful contingent rewards

Realities

- Difficult and time-consuming to implement performance–reward linkages, especially when linkages have not been made in the past
- Only worthwhile when sufficient rewards are at risk to be motivating
- Must successfully overcome rating leniency problems and managers' reticence to provide candid feedback
- Trust levels in the organization must be high for performance–reward linkages to be implemented successfully, and perceptions of fairness in making these linkages is essential
- Initially, no matter how well implemented, performance–reward linkages will be anxiety-provoking and are likely to decrease trust
- Performance–reward linkages increase manager's responsibilities and accountabilities
- Managers need training and organizational support to implement effectively

---

The underlying philosophy of linking performance and pay is to reward employees for the contributions and motivate performance through direct "line of sight" with rewards. Certainly, this is not a new idea, and many private sector organizations have linked performance and pay for years. However, organizations that traditionally have not linked performance and rewards are moving away from their traditional tenure-based systems in the direction of rewarding performance, to include many federal, state, and local government agencies, non-profit agencies, and international agencies. While linking performance and rewards sounds intuitively appealing and can have positive motivational effects, the complexities and difficulties associated with doing this, especially in organizations where these linkages have not been made traditionally, are significant.

Pay demonstration projects have shown that at least 2.5–4.5% of payroll needs to be at risk (e.g., in the form of bonuses) to have positive motivating effects. Further, to achieve optimal effects, significant contingent rewards should be available to the highest performing employees, for example, 10% of their salaries. However, in addition to having sufficient pay at risk, it is also essential that there is sufficient differentiation in ratings to support variable pay decisions that align with the ratings. For instance, if there is not differentiation in the ratings, it is not possible to justify significant differences in pay. The challenges associated with chronically lenient ratings discussed previously need to be successfully addressed for rewards to be effectively linked to performance. Managers need to get over any reticence they have to provide lower ratings and candid feedback to employees. The bottom line is that linking performance with rewards can be an effective practice, but it requires overcoming difficult challenges that are inherent in performance management processes.

Good to Know:
There's No Easy Way Out for Managers

If managers rate everyone at approximately the same level, they will indeed avoid having to give disappointing news to some employees. However, they will also need to explain to the truly effective performers, who are delivering substantially more than others, why they received exactly the same ratings and rewards as those who are contributing less. Either way, managers have to give bad news to someone. It's best that this not be to the most effective performers, because this will have de-motivating effects on the most productive workers – exactly the opposite of what was intended by implementing a system to reward performance.

Irrespective of how effectively a pay-for-performance system is initially implemented, there are several realities that should be expected. First, even in the healthiest organizations, any system that touches pay or other rewards is anxiety-producing. As a result, trust may initially decrease until the system is shown to be fair and procedurally just. To facilitate this, there needs to be standardized, transparent, and well-executed processes for translating performance measures into different levels of pay or other rewards. There also need to be a clear line of sight between what employees deliver and the outcomes they receive. Another final reality associated with linking performance and rewards is that managers have greater responsibility to ensure that performance management is done right, and organizations need to be prepared to support managers in their decisions. Managers need training as well as support from human resources and their managers when pay-for-performance processes are implemented.

Practical Training Exercises

Exercise 1:
Trust Building Exercise

Trainer Note. The purpose of this exercise is to teach trainees about behaviors that enhance trust between managers and employees. During the exercise, the checklist can be completed by managers regarding the extent to which they engage in trust building behaviors with their staff or by staff regarding the extent to which their managers engage in trust building behaviors with them. The procedures for the exercise need to be explained to participants before beginning:

- *Participants should not put their names on the rating form.*
- *After participants have completed the checklist, the completed forms should be passed in to the trainer, shuffled, and redistributed to trainees, such that no one knows whose sheet has been distributed to whom. Redistributing rating sheets to different participants protects the anonymity of respondents.*
- *The trainer should go through each item, ask the group to raise their hands if a check was placed next to that item on their sheet, and tally the responses.*
- *At a group level, this exercise provides feedback on the extent to which managers and/or employees report that managers are engaging in trust building behaviors, and it also identifies areas for improvement to increase trust.*

Trust Building Behavior Checklist Place a check in the appropriate box to the right of each statement, indicating the extent to which you engage in the following behaviors with your employees	Very great extent	Large extent	Moderate extent	Small extent	Not at all
1. I provide status reports and forecasts.					
2. I explain my priorities, unit priorities, and how these align with organizational priorities.					
3. I provide plausible explanations for actions that I take.					
4. I try to balance candor with discretion when communicating with my employees.					
5. I make realistic commitments and inform employees when things arise that prevent me from satisfying these.					
6. I let employees know when plans have changed, why they have changed, and the impact on them.					
7. I close the loop by letting people know when I have completed tasks I have said I would do.					
8. I show people that I have tried to develop win–win solutions to problems.					
9. I protect the interests of people who are not present by not criticizing them when they cannot defend themselves.					
10. I show compassion for employees, especially when a decision has negative consequences for them.					
11. I use probing and other communication techniques to verify people understand what I have told them.					
12. I admit my limits and do not promise more than I can deliver.					

Exercise 2:
Accomplishment Exercise

Trainer Note. The purpose of this exercise is to teach trainees how to write effective accomplishment statements. Participants will review three accomplishments and evaluate how well they are written against a checklist. The exercise can be conducted independently or in small groups, with a discussion following. Three example accomplishments appear below. These can be tailored to be more relevant to the organization in which training will occur.

Accomplishment Checklist

Write "Y" for Yes if the accomplishment satisfied the item and "N" for No if it did not.

Time Frame

_____ 1. Did the accomplishment occur within the current rating period?

Description of the Situation

_____ 2. Are the situation and circumstances the employee faced described?

_____ 3. Does the description provide sufficient context to understand what the employee accomplished or contributed?

Description of Specific Activities

_____ 4. Are the activities the employee performed described?

_____ 5. Are the activities described in sufficient detail so that readers can readily understand what was done?

_____ 6. Are the activities described in sufficient detail so that readers can understand why the activities were above and beyond typical performance expectations?

_____ 7. Did the employee describe his or her own specific activities, role, and responsibilities rather than team or group activities?

Description of Results/Impact

_____ 8. Does the accomplishment describe the results or outcome of the activities performed?

_____ 9. Does the accomplishment describe the specific impact that the contribution had on achievement of business or mission goals?

_____ 10. Is the impact described in sufficient detail so that readers outside the work unit will understand the significance of the accomplishment?

Overall Quality

_____ 11. Does the accomplishment contain correct spelling and grammar?

Example Accomplishment #1

Describe the situation and the activities you performed:
A junior employee in my branch was having trouble with a new assignment. I sat down to help her figure out why she was having difficulty. We identified a couple areas she could focus on, and found some training courses she could attend.

Describe the results and impact of your activities:
The employee attended all the training courses we identified for her.

Trainer Note: Items 3, 5, 6, 7, 8, 9, 10 on the checklist are missing or weak. A results statement was provided, but it does not speak to the critical outcome one would expect in this situation – development of skills, rather than merely attending training courses.

Example Accomplishment #2

Describe the situation and the activities you performed:
My office had six months before it transitioned to managing a new benefits program. I was very interested in leaning more about this area, so I volunteered to serve on the transition working group. I was selected to serve as the leader of the Customer Analysis team. I developed a plan for collecting input from employees regarding their needs and preferences for different potential benefits offerings. This plan included conducting focus groups, interviewing key stakeholders, and conducting a survey of employee needs. I coordinated all the focus groups and used the focus group results to develop the survey. I identified themes that the focus group participants had mentioned and wrote questions to measure their opinions about key topics. I researched different kinds of rating scales that can be used with surveys, learned about many different kinds, and selected the one I thought would meet our needs for information. I worked with other team members on the interviews, and implementation of the survey. I then analyzed the

Continued

data from the survey, and used Excel to create tables and charts that highlighted the interesting results. Finally, I organized and conducted a day-long team meeting to develop recommendations, and briefed the recommendations to the entire transition working group.

Describe the results and impact of your activities:
These activities resulted in the human resources department having good data upon which to base its decisions. We did not have to guess what our employees wanted, but instead could base our decisions on solid facts. As a result, employees reported high levels of satisfaction about how the benefits transition process was handled.

Trainer Note: Adequately addressed all items on the checklist.

Example Accomplishment #3

Describe the situation and the activities you performed:

- Our division had recently purchased a new human resources application with improved analysis and reporting capabilities that would allow us to serve our customers better.
- We were trying to transfer a database from the old application to the new one. We could not get the database to transfer properly. Sometimes data would be lost during the transfer, other times the relationships would be lost, or even worse, data would be rearranged. We worked on the problem for 10 days.
- Finally, one day before the deadline, I figured out how to make it work.

Describe the results and impact of your activities:

- The data were successfully transferred to the new application. This ensured accuracy of the data and ensured that everyone in the division could access needed data.
- The project was completed in a timely manner, before the deadline.
- Having the data in this new application allowed us to serve our customers better.

Trainer Note: Items 5, 6, 7, 10 on the checklist are all missing or weak. Although an impact statement was provided, the result on operations was unclear and more information would be desirable.

Exercise 3:
Writing Narratives Exercise

Trainer Note. This exercise is designed to help raters prepare more effective narrative comments. Participants review five examples of narrative comments and evaluate how well they meet guidelines for effective narrative comments. The exercise can be conducted independently or in small groups, with a group discussion following. The narratives in this exercise can be tailored to be more relevant to the performance standards that are being used in the organization where training is conducted.

Guidelines for Evaluating Rating Narratives

The purpose of narrative comments is to support particular ratings with specific, behavioral examples of employee performance. Effective narratives meet the following guidelines:

- Focus on job behaviors
  The primary function of narratives is to let others know what the employee has done that has led to a particular rating. The information included should directly support the rating *in terms of specific employee behaviors.* Unnecessary and inappropriate information (e.g., age, gender, medical problems, etc.) should not be included.
- Justify and support the rating given
  The narrative needs to be consistent with the rating given. For example, low ratings require that the narrative describe instances where the employee performed below standards. High ratings require the narrative to illustrate how the employee went beyond expectations.
- Provide sufficient detail
  Readers should have a clear understanding of why a particular rating was given.

For this exercise, assume that ratings were made on a 5-point scale, ranging from 1 = failed to meet expectations to 5 = exceeds expectations.

Continued

Example Narrative 1

Communicating with Others Meets Expectations Standards	Rating	Narrative
• Communicates complex concepts or ideas effectively in writing, so that readers who are unfamiliar with the topic or terminology can gain an understanding of key issues. • Proofs and edits documents to ensure the written message is accurate, clear, organized, and concise.	1	Pam never met the expectations for this standard. It is disappointing that Pam is not able to perform up to expectations for this performance standard. She needs training to improve her written communication skills.

Trainer Note: The comment basically repeats the information already conveyed in the rating: Pam is not performing up to expectations. The comment does not provide specific examples of when or how she failed to meet the expectations outlined in the standards.

Example Narrative 2

Collaborating with Others Meets Expectations Standards	Rating	Narrative
• Develops and maintains constructive, professional working relationships with others. • Displays and fosters an appreciation for the value of diversity in the workplace and treats all people with courtesy and respect. • Readily assists co-workers who encounter difficult tasks or situations. • Constructively manages interpersonal conflict, considering all parties' positions and working with them to come to a resolution.	2	I do not feel that Jan relates to others very well at all. It's not entirely Jan's fault that she does not interact well with her peers or subordinates very well; she is just very introverted and shy. Because of her personality, she has a hard time connecting with others. She is very quiet and withdrawn, and this makes it difficult for her to contribute to the team.

Trainer Note: Problematic narrative, because the comments should focus on Jan's behaviors rather than her introverted personality.

Continued

Example Narrative 3

Learning and Developing Exceeds Expectations Standards	Rating	Narrative
• Responds effectively and non-defensively to feedback about strengths and gaps that are important for own work. • Takes initiative to learn and apply new skills required to increase performance effectiveness. • Identifies training and learning opportunities on own, coordinates with manager, and fulfills development plan, resulting in enhanced skill acquisition and improved performance.	5	Tim has really done an outstanding job in terms of developing himself. At the beginning of the rating period, he came to me and asked my help in identifying an area for self-development that would really help his career progress. Together, Tim and I decided that he should focus on increasing his expertise in electronic publishing software. After choosing the area for development, Tim developed his own targeted plan, consisting of four different training and development activities. He has followed through in each of these areas and completed his development plan during the rating period. Tim is now the most skilled user of electronic publishing software in our unit.

Trainer Note: Good narrative, because it provides detailed examples of specific employee behaviors that met the "Exceeds Expectations" standards and led to rating of 5.

Example Narrative 4

Communicating with Others Exceeds Expectations Standards	Rating	Narrative
• Communicates ideas and information articulately, in a highly organized and logical fashion, and in a form well matched to the audience. • Responds to stated and implied questions in a clear, appropriate manner. • Enhances communications and delivery of information by using a range of appropriate presentation aids (e.g., graphs, charts, videos, slides); effectively utilizes computers and other technology to present information. • Responds appropriately to individual and group behavior in situations involving complex or sensitive issues; adapts on the spot to meet listener needs.	5	Last month, I had to leave unexpectedly for a family emergency. I asked Kim to fill in for me as a facilitator for a strategic planning session. I knew it would be a challenge for her, since I anticipated that the high-level meeting would be very difficult to facilitate. However, I thought she could handle it. She jumped in without hesitation to help out and handled the meeting well. A number of attendees complimented her on how she helped them focus and share their opinions.

Trainer Note: Problematic narrative, because it contains information that is irrelevant to this particular competency and focuses on a single instance of performance. Ratings should reflect typical performance over an entire rating period, and comments to justify the ratings should also cover the entire period.

Continued

Example Narrative 5

Technical Proficiency Meets Expectations Standards	Rating	Narrative
• Applies understanding of human resources business needs for data and manages data accordingly. • Applies business rules to enter appropriate information into human resources automated systems efficiently and accurately; proofs own and others' work, finding and correcting errors and ensuring that procedures are followed. • Updates and maintains files and records efficiently and accurately, organizing information to facilitate retrieval, • Efficiently retrieves appropriate information from commonly used record-keeping systems. • Completes administrative forms and paperwork accurately and in a timely manner.	2	Jane has not met expectations for this performance standard. There are a number of examples of her failure to do so. First, there were three separate occasions where she incorrectly forwarded the paperwork for assignments that she processed, and she also entered information into the automated human resources system incorrectly on six occasions. Also, Jane rarely completes her own paperwork on time. I have to track her down and ask her where various reports are at least once a month, and there has not been a single occasion when the reports have been finished when I have asked for them.

Trainer Note: Good narrative, which focuses on specific employees behaviors throughout the rating period that are relevant and tied well to the performance standards.

Example Exercise 4:
Performance Review Role Play

Trainer Note. The purpose of this exercise is to teach trainees that different people can have significantly different views about a situation and to provide practice in conducting effective performance feedback sessions. This exercise contains: (1) role play instructions for a manager, named Fisher; (2) role play instructions for an employee, named Wall; and (3) a checklist of behaviors that the manager and employee should exhibit during the feedback session. This exercise can be conducted in several ways, as follows:

- *One option is to have training participants break into pairs and conduct the role-play exercise. Following the role-play, the trainee playing the role of the employee rates the "manager" on how effectively he or she conducted the session, and the trainee playing the role of the manager rates the "employee" on how effectively he or she participated in the session.*
- *A second option is to have training participants break into groups of three. One participant plays the role of the manager, the second participant plays the role of the employee, and the third participant is the observer, rating the "manager" and the "employee" on how effectively they conducted the session.*
- *Another alternative is to have two trainers (or actors) demonstrate the role play, performing some aspects of the feedback session effectively and others ineffectively. Trainees observe the manager's and employee's performance, complete a checklist on how effectively they conducted the session, and then discuss their observations.*
- *The final alternative is to script roles and videotape actors playing the manager and employee roles. Specific effective and ineffective behaviors can be built into the videotapes. Trainees would complete the checklist regarding what the videotaped manager and employee did and did not do effectively and then discuss their observations.*

The option that should be selected depends on the situation. In some organizations, employees are reluctant to engage in role plays and do not find them credible. Also, if videotaped role-plays are used, there is maximum control over what behaviors are exhibited and more standardization in the learning points that can be built into the exercise. Irrespective of which option

Continued

is used, the general premise for the roles is presented below and performance should be evaluated using the provided checklists.

Role Play Exercise: Staff Member Role

In this exercise, you will play the role of an employee participating in a performance discussion with your manager. You will find a description of the overall work situation, and a description of your character's thoughts about what should be discussed. Please stick to the basic facts outlined in the scenario, but feel free to improvise within the framework. The role play should take about 10–15 minutes. When everyone is finished, we will get back together as a group and discuss lessons learned.

Background – Staff Member Role

You are T. Wall. You work with 15 other staff and get along very well with all of them. Your group is one of the most productive. People get along really well and support each other. You are very skilled in doing technical work and enjoy it – you have always been one of the best. You are also an extremely good technical mentor and teacher. The people in your group have a reputation for being the best because of the training you provide. They are sought after regularly by others. You know this because your staff members are frequently selected to take challenging jobs in other parts of the organization.

Your group is one of several in a division. People in the division are also team-oriented and productive, although many of the other group leaders aren't as good technically as you are. When you first joined the organization, you regularly jumped in to help your peers on technical problems they were facing. You soon found that you had become the "go to" guy and many people came to you for advice on their technical problems. While you really liked serving in this technical guru role, the people on your team started feeling neglected and told you that they weren't getting enough of your time. So you had to cut back in helping other team leaders to make sure you had enough time for your team.

Your manager, S.A. Fisher distributes the work pretty much as it comes in. Because your team is one of the most productive and technically proficient, you tend to receive more work than others.

You and your team pride yourselves in being able to take on many projects and the most difficult ones. To make sure your people get the best training possible, you have been lobbying for the most difficult and innovative projects to be given to your group. You feel strongly that the only way your staff members are going to learn is to make them perform the most challenging projects. This strategy has worked really well because your team is, in fact, the best. Since you have been lobbying for the most challenging work, Fisher has come through and given your group very interesting assignments, but has not always seemed happy about this.

Although you have had a very successful and productive year, there was one incident recently that bothered you that you may bring up with Fisher. In a customer meeting, you proposed doing something differently that had not occurred to you before. Because the thought did not come to you until the meeting, you did not pre-coordinate your idea with Brown, the project director. However, you got so excited about this that you went ahead and shared your thoughts with the group. There was a change in the customer's direction as a result of your suggestion and some additional work that Brown had to do. Nonetheless, your idea is going to make a very important improvement in the work. Brown was furious about your not pre-coordinating with him – unreasonably so, under the circumstances. Although you apologized to Brown and offered to help with the additional work, Brown was upset and made a really big deal about doing something that everyone agreed was better for the project.

Today, Fisher has asked to get together. It should not take very long, and it will be nice to hear again about the good work you are doing.

Role Play Exercise: Manager Role

In this exercise, you will play the role of a manager conducting a performance discussion with a staff member. You will find a description of the overall work situation, and a description of your character's thoughts about what should be discussed in the review session. Please stick to the basic facts outlined in the scenario, but feel free to improvise within the framework. The role play itself should take about 10–15 minutes. When everyone is finished, we will get back together as a group and discuss the lessons learned.

Continued

Background – Manager's Role

You are S.A. Fisher, a manager, with 15 staff reporting to you. Today, you have arranged to meet with one of them, T. Wall, for a performance discussion.

Overall, Wall is exceptional technically. He is part of a very hard-working, productive unit. However, Wall's cooperation with others has a lot to be desired. When first in the unit, Wall was extremely helpful and pitched in to provide assistance whenever anyone needed it. Gradually, Wall has become less and less helpful to others. You have asked other team members to talk over technical issues with Wall, but they tell you that Wall refuses to help and even makes sarcastic remarks that they can't do their own work. On one occasion, Wall blind-sided Brown, a co-worker, by not pre-coordinating on a suggestion that Wall made directly to Brown's customer. You expect staff to keep each other informed and cooperate such things.

In addition, Wall recently refused to take on two assignments, saying that they were too easy and low level for his group. Wall wants the most challenging and difficult work and asked you to give the routine assignments to others. You had plenty of work to go around, so you granted the request. But, you can't continue giving Wall the most interesting work without causing problems for others. Also, if Wall is not going to help others, it's not right to reward Wall with the best projects. You've decided to meet today to discuss this matter and your general concerns about the lack of cooperation you have seen.

Wall's failure to cooperate has you worried for another reason. There has been a lot of turnover among junior staff who work with Wall. You have heard no complaints yet, but you are wondering if Wall is treating junior staff poorly. Certainly, if Wall is stubborn and uncooperative with others, this same behavior may be occurring with junior staff.

You want to discuss these issues with Wall today to try and resolve things before they get further out of hand.

Performance Review Session Checklist for the Manager

Check each item that applies:

- Explained the purpose of the meeting
  - —— Indicated that the meeting was a discussion of the employee's performance
  - —— Outlined the topics to be covered in meeting

- Maintained open, two-way dialogue with employee
  —— Asked employee for his/her opinion on how the job is going
  —— Asked employee for ideas on strengths and developmental needs
  —— Allowed employee to speak when he/she had something to say
  —— Asked employee for opinions, questions, concerns
- Recognized employee's achievements
  —— Praised employee for good work observed over the rating period
  —— Highlighted areas where employee has done particularly well
- Discussed developmental needs with employee in a constructive manner
  —— Identified specific problem behaviors
  —— Focused on behaviors rather than personality traits
  —— Listened and responded to employee's comments about these areas
  —— Interacted in a professional, constructive manner
- Worked with employee to develop plan of action
  —— Asked for employee's opinion on course of action to take
  —— Helped employee set attainable goals in terms of specific actions
  —— Identified ideas to help the employee address issues
  —— Created a timeline for steps he/she and employee would take to achieve plan

Performance Review Session Checklist for the Employee

Check each item that applies:

- Listened openly to the feedback
  —— Actively listened to what supervisor was saying
  —— Paraphrased what had been said to ensure understanding
  —— Asked questions when appropriate
- Treated review session as opportunity to learn
  —— Interacted in a professional, non-defensive manner
  —— Cooperated with supervisor
- Actively participated in identifying developmental needs and a plan
  —— Professionally explained his/her view of the situation
  —— Recognized that he/she has areas for improvement
  —— Set challenging, realistic goals
  —— Indicated willingness and made commitments to work on improving

Chapter 5

Performance Management System Implementation

Having an effective performance management process and tools is a necessary, but not sufficient condition for effective performance management. What really matters with any performance management system is how seriously it is taken and how conscientiously it is used by managers and employees. This is why both the most challenging and the most important part of developing an effective performance management system is implementation. In Chapter 3, several best practices relevant to implementation were discussed as important for laying the groundwork for a new system. These included:

- Ensuring there is sufficient leadership support for the system
- Gaining buy-in for the system from staff at all levels
- Realistically assessing the organization's appetite for performance management
- Developing an effective communications strategy

Once the performance management tools and processes have been designed, several additional implementation steps are necessary. These include automating the tools and processes to the extent possible, pilot testing, training staff on using the system, evaluating the system, and improving the system based on the evaluation results. The following sections discuss best practices relevant to these implementation steps. They are derived from organizational change principles, best practices studies, and the views of experienced practitioners about how to successfully implement performance management systems.

Tips:
Cornerstones of Successful Post-Design Implementation

- Automate as much as possible
- Implement an appeals process
- Pilot test the system prior to large-scale implementation
- Train employees and managers on all aspects of the system and process
- Evaluate and continually improve the system based on evaluation results

Practical Exercise

At the end of this chapter, practical Training Exercise 5 can be used to help to engage and empower managers and staff in the implementation process.

Automation of Performance Management Processes

Organizations have had a long history of attempting to increase work efficiency and effectiveness. From the advent of repetitive flow production in the early 1900s, to the use of Total Quality Management in the 1980s, to the recent trend to outsource non-mission critical functions, organizations continually strive to increase their effectiveness through increased efficiency. This has recently resulted in widespread implementation of automated Human Resource Information Systems (HRIS), whose purpose is to more efficiently deliver human resource-related business functions. Vendors such as SAP, People-Soft, and Oracle offer HRIS that allow employers to track and manage employees as they move through the employment lifecycle from pre- to post-hire. Typically, these systems automate human resource functions, such as time and attendance, leave, benefits, pay, recruiting, and staffing.[1] Performance management functions have also been integrated into these large HRIS as more tools and platforms have become available that automate the appraisal process.

Functionality Provided by Automated Systems

Evaluations of automated performance management systems have shown that they are viewed positively by users overall, decrease workload, ensure widespread access, and provide a standardized format for collecting, storing, and reporting performance data.

Example:
Basic Level of Functionality in Automated System

- User interfaces for displaying competencies, performance standards, and performance management process information
- Make and capture performance ratings
- Web pages that contain help, information, and instruction files

---

To make informed decisions about the extent of automation beyond the basic functions, time, resources, development, and maintenance costs need to be considered. For example, database development and maintenance represent significant costs beyond applications development. Additionally, features such as information security, archiving, and records management represent areas that require additional consideration. There are a variety of advanced features that can be built into an automated performance management system, including:

- *Capturing input from multiple rating sources.* Automated performance management systems have proven to be invaluable for the implementation of multi-source or 360-degree feedback systems, which are inherently more complex from an administrative standpoint than managerial evaluations. First, several raters must be selected from multiple rating sources (e.g., peers, customers) from which feedback is sought. With the exception of the manager, a minimum of three raters from each source are needed to provide feedback. Since not all potential raters provide feedback when they are asked, it is necessary to ask for feedback from more than the minimum needed. Usually, at least five to six raters from each ratings source are asked. This means that if feedback is sought from three sources (peers, direct reports, and customers), requests will need to be sent and rating forms made available to approximately 15–18 raters per employee. Once completed, the ratings from these different participants need to be compiled and analyzed by rating source (e.g., all peer ratings combined). A feedback report is then generated showing the results. Automated systems are almost essential for this type of multi-rater application, allowing for efficient selection of raters, easy access to rating forms, collection and analysis of data from multiple sources, and automated development and delivery of reports.[2]

- *Capturing employee input.* This includes capturing accomplishments and any other types of employee input (e.g., comments, ratings) on-line.
- *Managing workflow.* This includes prompting managers, employees, reviewers, and human resources staff about deadlines relevant to the performance management process and providing access to forms and documents that are needed during the process.
- *Providing automated feedback and training to managers.* The goal of this feedback is to help managers and other raters mitigate rating inflation and other rating errors that commonly occur when one individual evaluates the performance of another. For example, an automated system can be programmed to track and analyze managers' ratings over time. When sufficient data have been collected on a large enough group of employees (e.g., 50–100), managers whose ratings seem to exhibit certain patterns (e.g., constantly rating employees at the highest rating levels) can be given feedback on their ratings and reminded to make sure their ratings reflect both strengths and development needs. Alternatively, managers' ratings can also be evaluated and feedback provided in real time as they are making them. This can be accomplished by flagging ratings of an employee that meet certain predetermined thresholds and prompting managers to review their ratings for accuracy. For example, ratings might be flagged when an employee is rated at exactly the same level on all of the competencies or when an employee receives an average rating of 4.75 or above on a 5-point scale, which may be unrealistically high, or a rating of 2.25 or below, which may be unrealistically low.
- *Reporting.* This capability involves generating automated reports at preprogrammed intervals to track system effectiveness. For example,

reports can be produced showing the average ratings by competency, division, department, group, or other relevant entity. Similarly, ratings for protected demographic groups (e.g., employees over 40, minority groups) compared to non-protected groups can be regularly examined for adverse impact or other issues of concern. As another example, reports can be produced that show the relationships between performance ratings and outcomes such as pay and promotion. All of these types of reports are beneficial to produce on an ongoing basis, because they provide useful information about the health of a performance management system and enable timely interventions to address any problems.

- *Providing evaluation support tools.* Evaluation support tools include such things as sample behavioral statements that can be used to develop narratives, developmental activities that can be pursued to enhance performance on each competency, example performance objectives, and any other information that may facilitate completion of the appraisal. The idea is that such examples provide models and starting points for developing narratives, objectives, etc., which should increase efficiency, effectiveness, and standardization across different managers.

- *Development and training support.* Some software allows employees to create, store, and monitor their progress in achieving their individual development plans. Other related functionality includes the ability to request and get approval for formal training and to register for training programs.

- *Facilitating HR decision-making.* Software tools can also be implemented to facilitate making compensation and other human resources decisions. Once managers finalize employees' ratings, they can be automatically plotted on a graph that shows where each employee stands within their job level. Taking into account the employee's performance ratings, the tool helps managers identify which employees might be under- or over-paid for their job category and level of performance. Managers can also experiment with alternative compensation amounts for different employees, while tracking the overall impact of these decisions on payroll. Other functionality allows importing performance evaluations so that they can be used with additional information to facilitate succession planning, staffing, and other human resources functions.

Buy versus Build Decision

The first step in deciding what automation features should be included in a system is to collect user requirements. This involves querying relevant constituencies within an organization to identify what automated functions are needed and desirable. Since different groups typically have somewhat different needs and desires, requirements should minimally be collected from the perspective of the organization's leadership, human resources department, IT department, performance management reviewers, managers, and employees. It is also important to examine commercial-off-the-shelf (COTS) products to learn about the different types of functionality that are available in the marketplace and to assess the costs of different software options.

A key decision that needs to be made is whether to buy a commercial product or to design and build an in-house product. Use of commercial products requires entering into licensing agreements where organizations are charged for using the products. The advantage of commercial products is that they can usually be implemented quickly (relative to an in-house development project), and they are maintained and updated by the developer over time. The biggest potential downside of commercially available software is that licensing agreements last in perpetuity and can be expensive.

Some commercial products provide a performance management shell and the organization provides the content (e.g., competencies, performance standards, and so forth). Other products provide both automated functionality and performance management content. In either case, if an organization wishes to use a commercially available product, it is important to use a reputable vendor, preferably one that is stable and will remain in business.

Use of a vendor with human resources system development expertise is especially important if the organization plans to use a process, competencies, or performance standards provided by the vendor. The concern here is whether or not a vendor's generically developed competencies and performance standards will be job-relevant or valid for use with a given organization's jobs. In this situation, not only is software development expertise important but expertise is needed in the development and implementation of valid and defensible performance management systems. Ideally, the vendor should have industrial and organizational psychologists, who specialize in this area.

As an alternative to using commercial products, organizations may opt to develop their own automated performance management tools. Ownership of the automated platform eliminates the need to pay a licensing fee but the organization then has the responsibility for updating and maintaining the system. For instance, it would be necessary to maintain databases of ratings, analyze and report data for decision-making, and periodically revise the system. With a number of high quality and high functionality tools available on the market, most organizations today are opting to purchase a performance management platform but develop their own customized and validated content to be used within these.

Potential Consequences of Automation

While automation of performance management processes has produced largely positive results, there are some potential negative consequences as well. On the positive side, non-automated systems tend to be paper-intensive and require passing documents through many people, from the manager, to a reviewer, to the employee, back to the manager, and eventually to human resources. Automation greatly streamlines the performance management workflow by enabling documents to be accessed electronically by different parties. It also substantially reduces paperwork by enabling completion and storage of information on-line rather than in paper form, thus providing an easily accessible repository of information. While this facilitates human resources data collection, decision-making, and reporting, such readily assessable data also allows for easy analysis of performance management and other human resources information, including investigation of adverse impact. Many human resources professionals anticipate increasing litigation as a result of having readily accessible data available in automated systems. In the past, it was difficult and time-consuming to compile records and conduct the data analyses that were necessary to evaluate system effectiveness and potential legal issues. However, data stored in automated systems is easy to retrieve and thoroughly analyze, increasing the potential for finding problems and reinforcing the importance of conducting performance management and other human resources activities in accordance with legal and professional standards.

Another expected advantage of automation is that the process efficiencies it affords should free up time for managers and employees to engage in more useful performance management activities, such as performance conversations and developmental activities, rather than paperwork. A cautionary note, however, is that by making evaluations easier to complete and process, automation may tempt managers to get their performance management responsibilities done as quickly as possible, focusing their efforts on on-line activities rather than engaging with employees. Another potential downside of automation occurs when the system includes tools that are intended to be helpful to managers but can also be misused, such as example

---

Case Scenario:
Do Managers Customize Narratives when Example Comments Are Available in Automated Systems?

A commercially available automated performance management system offered sample narrative comments for different levels of performance effectiveness. A large information technology company and a large retail sales organization were both considering implementation of this feature. However, both had concerns about making example comments available because they thought the managers might produce "cookie cutter" narratives for their employees, using the comments verbatim rather then customizing the narratives to reflect what the employee actually did. If this happened, employees might be turned off by the lack of personalization in the narratives. They might also perceive a lack of interest in performance management on the part of their managers. The feature was implemented on a trial basis. Evaluations of the narratives showed that managers did, in fact, customize the generic text to make it applicable for individual employees. The managers felt that the availability of example comments was very helpful in preparing their reviews, increasing both efficiency and consistency. Because the generic comments were customized to be meaningful to individual employees, employees also had positive reactions to their narratives.

narrative statements. If managers use these directly without taking the time to edit them so they are meaningful for staff, the performance management process may become mechanical and lose credibility. The bottom line, however, is that the advantages of automated tools and the advanced functionality they provide almost always outweigh potential concerns and disadvantages.

Implement an Appeals Process

It is important to include an appeals process in any performance management system because this gives the organization an opportunity to learn about and deal with potential problems before they escalate into formal challenges. Having an appeals process in place also helps to increase employees' perceptions of fairness regarding the system. Appeals processes take different forms in different organizations. Some have separate committees that hear, investigate, and decide on appeals. Others handle this process through the human resources department. Irrespective of the mechanisms and specific processes for handling appeals, the important point is to develop and implement a formal process where employee can safely and objectively have any concerns about their evaluations reviewed and addressed.

Pilot Test

Another important factor in ensuring a successful implementation is to pilot test a new process in a few units prior to large-scale implementation. Pilot testing helps diagnose whether or not a system is functioning properly and illuminates areas for revision prior to going live. It also provides useful information about whether managers and employees understand and support the process and if further change-management or communication efforts are needed. Importantly, a pilot test provides an opportunity to gauge reactions to the system and make adjustments that will facilitate acceptance.

Pilot testing should include all aspects of the system – the automated system, performance management content, written materials, training programs, and the assignment and analysis of ratings. What this means is that a full pilot test will be resource- and time-intensive, something that can be unappealing to organizational decision-makers who often want fast implementation. In fact, it is sometimes difficult to convince decision-makers who want to expedite implementation about the value of pilot testing. However, the negative attitudes and irrecoverable bad press that a failed system roll-out can produce – for example, the automated system crashing – are simply not worth the time gained or risk associated with forgoing a pilot test.

Train Employees and Managers

Employees and managers need to be able and motivated to conduct performance management effectively. Training helps to accomplish both of these objectives. There are different types of training that can be used for performance management – classroom training, job aides, or web-based training. The training format and strategy that make the most sense in a given situation depend on the extent of buy-in there is for the system, how much employees and managers already engage in effective performance management, and the resources – both time and financial – that the organization is willing to invest in the training process.

Performance management is an area where practice and feedback are particularly useful for learning. Because of the interactive nature of many performance management activities, the most effective type of training is classroom training, where trainees participate in a variety of exercises to teach and reinforce key learning objectives. For example, experienced practitioners have found that there is no comparison for classroom training when the topic is how to give and receive feedback, because this venue allows trainees to practice and grow more comfortable with the feedback, coaching, and development process. In addition, when an organization devotes the time and resources that are required for large-scale classroom training, a very strong message about the importance of performance management is sent to employees. The type of training provided and requirement or lack thereof to attend training communicate a great deal to employees about leadership's commitment to performance management.

If an organization elects to provide classroom training, there are usually training programs for managers and employees that are offered at several points during the performance management cycle. While different training programs could be developed for these different audiences, an advantage of using the same training content for both is that everyone receives the same information, which helps to increase trust in how the system will be implemented. Although the training content for managers and employees can be identical or very similar, it is best to conduct separate training sessions for these two audiences. This is because lower-level employees can be reticent about participating in training when managers are in the same session.

To enhance transfer of training to the job, it is best to provide training on each major step of the performance management process immediately before managers and employees need to perform that step, as this helps to ensure relevant information is fresh in their minds. While this requires a larger number of training sessions overall, the sessions are shorter and more focused than if all of the content is taught in one session. Experience in several organizations has shown that employees and managers prefer and find it more meaningful to attend one or two hour sessions at different points during the year rather than a full-day or more of training prior to implementation. A proposed set of classroom training sessions and timeframes for conducting these is shown in the example.

Example:
Proposed Classroom Training Sessions and Timing

- Training Session 1: General roll-out and overview of the system and setting performance objectives – one month prior to implementation
- Training Session 2: Having effective performance conversations – within approximately the first month of the performance management cycle
- Training Session 3: Preparing accomplishments, rating performance, and having formal review sessions – one month before accomplishments are due

---

An alternative to classroom training is web-based training. Simple web-based training programs can be developed to teach the mechanics of a performance management process or more advanced training can be developed that provides practice exercises and feedback. The advantage of web-based training is that participants can complete the training at their own pace and don't have to physically attend a program outside their office. These advantages are also the precise disadvantages of this type of training. Because participants are not required to physically attend a scheduled session, they can procrastinate taking the training, ignore it altogether, or race through it just to get it done. If a web-based training approach is going to work well, it usually requires policing to make sure that employees take the training and acquire the needed skills. Although web-based training is viewed as more efficient, flexible, and cost-effective over time, customized web-based training programs can be very expensive to develop, especially if they include interactive practice exercises. Beyond the cost, however, the more important question is whether or not a web-based approach will result in the learning and motivation that are necessary to effectively use the new system.

Shown in the example is a comprehensive list of performance management training topics. For many of these topics, exercises that provide practice or feedback to trainees can be included. Because adult learning principles focus on the importance of experiential learning, lecture content should be minimized and exercise content maximized. Throughout this book are exercises that can be used to reinforce learning in several areas.

Example:
Performance Management Training Topics

- Philosophy and purposes for which system will be used
- Plan for rolling out and educating organizational members about the system
- Roles and responsibilities of leaders, reviewers, feedback providers, managers, employees and human resources
- Major components of the performance management system and process
- Rationale for and review of performance standards
- How to discuss expectations and set performance objectives
- The importance of ongoing, constructive, and specific behavioral feedback
- How to seek feedback effectively from others
- How to react to and act on feedback in a constructive manner
- How to give feedback to minimize defensiveness and maintain self-esteem
- How to build trust between managers and staff

- How to gather effective feedback from other rating sources
- How to prepare summaries of your most meritorious accomplishments
- How to provide accurate evaluations that minimize rating errors and rating inflation
- How to work with other managers to ensure uniform application of standards and consistency in ratings
- How to prepare effective rating narratives
- How to conduct effective formal review sessions
- How to provide effective coaching and mentoring
- How to identify and address development needs
- How to address disciplinary or serious performance problems
- How to link performance ratings to outcomes (if applicable)
- How to use the automated system and related software
- How to monitor, evaluate, and improve the performance management system over time

Performance management learning aids can be used to support more formal approaches to training. The advantage of such aids is that they can be made available on-line and used whenever an employee needs to be refreshed on some part of the system. For example, an aid might be developed that helps managers write good performance objectives or one might be developed that summarizes the key performance management activities and schedule. Performance management learning aids are useful once employees have participated in formal training and have experience with the performance management process. However, they are not sufficient as the sole basis for training and certainly do not provide the practice and feedback that are needed to perform performance management activities well.

Tips:
Consider Providing a Performance Management Hotline

- Managers and employees can call in to ask questions about the process
- Particularly useful during the time period when major performance management activities occur (e.g., setting objectives, writing accomplishments, rating performance, etc.) but cannot be used in lieu of training
- Important to ensure that the hotline is adequately staffed so that employees' and managers' questions are responsively addressed

Evaluate and Continually Improve the System

Performance management systems should be evaluated and continually improved over time. If data are stored in an automated system, a number of measures can be easily collected and reviewed on a regular basis. Other measures, for example, assessments of user satisfaction with the system, require separate data collections. Since different measures provide information on how different aspects of the system are working, it is best to track and collect a number of measures in order to obtain a complete picture of overall system effectiveness. The following practices are encouraged:

- *Monitor Completion of Training:* This involves verifying that all users of the performance management system have received training prior to implementation.
- *Monitor Completion of Appraisals:* This involves verifying that performance appraisal ratings have been completed and signed off on by managers, employees, and other required persons, such as human resources.

Assess Quality Using a Formal Performance Management Review

This is the process where a higher level manager or human resources staff member reviews each employee's package to ensure that:

- Narrative comments are aligned with and support the ratings
- Ratings do not appear positively or negatively biased
- Especially high or low ratings have been properly justified
- Evaluation criteria appear to be applied systematically across supervisors and employees
- Proper distinctions have been made between employees, based on their performance and contributions

Assess Alignment with Related HR Decisions

If a performance management system is used as a basis for pay, promotion, or reductions in force, the consistency between the evaluations and outcomes received needs to be monitored. For example,

---

Good to Know:
Rating Calibration Helps Ensure an Effective Performance Management Process

It is good practice for managers in a given unit to meet, discuss the ratings for all employees, and together decide on the final rank-ordering or groupings of staff for decision-making purposes.

- Primary advantage – it helps to ensure that consistent distinctions are made between employees who are exceeding, meeting, or falling below expectations. The reason is that managers end up discussing specific examples of performance in relation to the standards, which helps them develop consensus about how to interpret and apply them.

- Primary disadvantage – while a consensus process facilitates more systematic decision-making, it is less practical and effective in situations where managers are geographically dispersed or lack familiarity with the performance of many employees in the group.

---

those who receive the highest numerical ratings should receive higher levels of pay and those who receive the lowest ratings should be the first to be let go in a reduction in force. Assessing the alignment between performance ratings and outcome decisions is facilitated if data are collected and analyzed in an automated system.

Evaluate User Reactions

Surveys or focus groups should be used periodically to collect user reactions to and satisfaction with the performance management process. Modifications can then focus on areas that are viewed as less effective by users. One strategy that not only gathers useful information but also serves as a catalyst for increasing performance discussions is to survey organizational members on the extent to which they are seeking, giving, and receiving feedback. Experienced practitioners have found that reporting these results back to managers and employees can increase the frequency and quality feedback that is exchanged over time.[3]

Example:
Performance Management Monitoring Procedures and Metrics

- Gather comments about concerns users have
  - Provide an open web-site for comments that are regularly reviewed
  - Periodically conduct focus group feedback sessions
  - Dedicate a task force to review comments/feedback and make suggestions for improvement
  - Monitor and categorize comments received by the help line
- Survey employees and managers about their performance management attitudes
  - Are the appraisals helpful? Accurate? Useful for making decisions?
  - Is feedback being given? Received? Sought?
  - Are individual performance objectives being set? Are they challenging but achievable?
  - Are expectations being communicated? Are they clear? Are there linkages between individual goals and higher-level goals?
  - Are the rating standards useful?
  - Are employees preparing accomplishment statements?
  - Are employees and managers able to easily integrate performance management processes into their work life, or is the system too burdensome?
  - Are managers taking performance management seriously or brushing it aside?
  - Does performance management help achieve business results?
  - Is performance management helpful for getting work done?
- Survey employees and managers about development
  - Are employees being pushed to strengthen their skills? To specialize?
  - Are development goals being, set? Monitored? Achieved?
  - Are employees counseled on career options based on their capabilities and interests?
  - Is the Development Resource being used?
  - Are employees devoting time to meeting the goals on their individual development plans?
  - Are employees meeting their development goals?

- Evaluate system records
  - Are performance objectives finalized and recorded on time?
  - Are performance appraisal ratings and development plans completed and submitted on time?
  - What proportion of employees have attended performance management training?
  - How many grievances have been filed?
  - Is the organization or employees prevailing in grievance matters?
  - How much are grievances and associated work costing the organization?
- Evaluate a sample of completed rating forms
  - Are the performance objectives meaningful, well defined, and measurable?
  - Are objectives tied to validated work behaviors or performance standards?
  - Are objectives similarly difficult and complex for employees in the same job?
  - Are forms being periodically updated as people achieve their goals or circumstances change?
  - Are accomplishment statements being completed?
  - Do rating narratives align with the ratings? Are they behavioral? Useful? Provide good documentation for especially high or low ratings? Clear to outside readers?
  - Do accomplishment statements meet all of the criteria for good accomplishments?
  - Are all development activities oriented around taking training classes only, or do they reflect on-the-job experiences and other learning activities?
  - Do development plans reflect experiences from the Development Resource?
- Analyze rating data
  - Examine rating averages and distributions – most ratings should be around the center of the scale ("Meets Expectations") and with reasonable differentiation between employees
  - Look at average rating scores and distributions across work groups
  - Look at average rating scores and distributions of ratings by race/gender group to evaluate equivalency of ratings across groups
  - Look at average rating scores and distributions of ratings by competency – lower averages on some competencies might mean training is needed organization-wide
  - Look at whether or not the rewards received align with the ratings given

Practical Exercise

Example Exercise 5:
Implementation Discussion Exercise

Trainer Note: The purpose of this exercise to get organizational members thinking about ways they can contribute to effective performance management implementation and solve implementation problems. Divide the class into three groups. Each will discuss a separate issue that may impact the performance management implementation success. The groups should be no more than 10–12 participants. If the training class is bigger than 30, you may divide into a larger number of groups, and some will discuss the same issue.

Assign an issue to each group. The discussions should last about 20 minutes. Trainees should not only discuss the issues but they should also brainstorm strategies and practical solutions to address them. Each group should appoint someone to record the group's conclusions on a flip chart. One group member will also need to report out for the group.

Issue 1

- What are the biggest concerns among employees about the new direction for performance management and what can be done to address these?

Issue 2

- What are the biggest concerns among managers about the new direction for performance management and what can be done to address these?

Issue 3

- What organizational barriers exist to implementing the new performance management system and what can be done to address these?

Part III

How to Develop Solid Performance Measures

Chapter 6

Legal Requirements

W̲e begin this part with a discussion of legal issues because there are well-articulated legal and professional guidelines that govern the development of measures that are used to assess job performance in work situations. Equal employment opportunity and fair employment practice laws, such as Title VII of the Civil Rights Act and the Equal Pay Act, make it possible to challenge employment decisions. While litigation related to employment practices has occurred for over 30 years, its incidence has recently proliferated.[1] These challenges can result in jury trials, compensatory or punitive damages, and high-profile class action lawsuits. Legal requirements are relevant to performance management when appraisals are used as a basis for decision-making, such as pay, bonuses, promotions, or reductions in force. As a result, they can be the subject of employment litigation. Both the results of a performance management process (i.e., the ratings) as well as procedural aspects of performance management systems can be challenged. As examples, challenges can be targeted at the specificity or subjectivity of performance criteria, standardization of operational procedures, or lack of internal consistency (for example, ratings that do not differentiate well between employees but pay increases and bonus awards that do), among other things.

Good to Know:
The Likelihood of Challenges to Performance
Management Systems Is High

Employment challenges have proliferated to the point that it is almost guaranteed that some aspect of an organization's performance manage- ment process will be challenged eventually, and it is likely that it will be the focus of a lawsuit at some point in time.

There are two main types of challenges that can be made against an organization's performance management system. The first is called a disparate treatment case, the second is the disparate impact case. In a disparate treatment case, the employee is claiming that she or he was treated differently by an employer than other employees who were in a similar situation. For example, assume both Mary and Jim failed to come to work one day, and the employer fires Mary but not Jim. If the reason the employer fired Mary was because she is female, then this is unlawful because the decision was based on the gender of the employee. If Mary was fired was because she had consistently bad attendance, this could be disparate treatment due to differences in Mary and Jim's attendance records. However, this would be lawful.

In a disparate impact case, the claim is that the employer has a practice that systematically and negatively impacts an entire group, for example, the employer won't hire individuals unless they have college degrees. This practice might have a much larger impact on minority candidates as a whole than it has on white candidates as a whole, such that the requirement for a degree results in significantly less minorities being hired than whites. To summarize, then, a disparate treatment challenge concerns how a specific individual was treated, while a disparate impact challenge claims that an organization's system or process systematically discriminates against a protected class of people (e.g., females, disabled persons, people over 40, African Americans, etc.). While disparate treatment has been conceptualized as an individual claim, it has been recognized by the courts in class actions. The payoff to plaintiffs is much higher in disparate treatment claims (i.e., punitive damages) so they have been increasingly weaving these arguments into cases, as early as the 1990s. A recent article from the American Bar Association (http://www.abanet.org/irr/hr/spring04/forced.html) discusses the use of disparate treatment arguments as part of the class actions on age in performance management.

While any type of challenge is time-consuming and can be expensive, class action lawsuits can result in significant monetary damages and can last literally decades. In addition, if a human resources system is found to be faulty as a result of a lawsuit, the organization may be required as part of the settlement to implement significant changes to the system. These are often overseen by court-appointed outside experts. In this situation, organizations can lose control of their own human resources systems and be required to implement what is directed by the outside expert group. Thus, not only can litigation be expensive and time-consuming, but it can result in outsiders playing a significant role in the design and oversight of an organization's human resources systems and processes.

Organizational leaders sometimes need to be made aware of the potential for legal challenges and their consequences. There are specific steps that need to be taken to be able to defend a performance management system if it is challenged. These steps require additional work, time, and resources. Especially when there is a desire to get a new system implemented quickly, there can be pressure to forgo the additional work that is required to address legal concerns, especially if leaders view the chances of being challenged as very small. More than one organization's leaders have made the decision not to be overly concerned about legal requirements, only to suffer significant legal problems later on. It is therefore important that organizational leaders understand the legal requirements and possible risks so that they can make fully informed decisions about how to develop and use their human resources systems.

Because performance management is a frequent focus in employment litigation matters, it is important to be familiar with the laws and professional guidelines that apply to the design and implementation of these systems. While an in-depth discussion of legal issues and comprehensive review of associated case law is beyond the scope of

	Case Scenario:
	No One is Immune to Legal Challenges

Many organizations feel that they are immune to legal challenges, especially if they have not experienced them in the past. One information technology organization, where everyone was doing very well financially because they had stock options, explicitly stated they were not worried about legal challenges because everyone was so happy to be there. Within five years, the organization faced a class action lawsuit, alleging discrimination in the allocation of performance-based rewards. Because they had not been worried about legal challenges, they had not taken steps to ensure that their performance management processes, which were used to make rewards decisions, could be defended. In the end, this organization, where leaders were convinced they would never have a legal challenge – let alone lose – lost the lawsuit and had to pay very substantial damages to the class.

this book, numerous resources are available for obtaining this information, including:

- Kahn, S. C., Brown, B. B., & Lanzarone, M. (1996). *Legal guide to human resources.* Boston: Warren, Gorham & Lamont, 6–2 to 6–58.
- Malos, S. (1998). Current legal issues in performance appraisal. In J.W. Smither (Ed.), *Performance appraisal: State of the art in practice* (pp. 49–94). San Francisco: Jossey-Bass.
- Malos, S. (2005). The importance of valid selection and performance appraisal: do management practices figure in case law? In F.J. Landy (Ed.), *Employment discrimination litigation* (pp. 373–409). San Francisco: Jossey-Bass.
- Martin, D. C., Bartol, K.M., & Kehoe, P. E. (2000). The legal ramifications of performance appraisal: The growing significance. *Public Personnel Management*, 29(3), 379–406.

Shown below is a brief summary of guidelines derived from case law and professional practice standards that are important in defending an organization's performance management practices.

Tips:
How to Address Legal Requirements

- Performance measures must be based on job-relevant factors
- Employees need to be clearly told what they are expected to do, what they are expected to accomplish, and what standards will be used for evaluation
- Specific roles, responsibilities, and timeframes for accomplishing performance management activities must be defined and well documented for managers and employees
- Training should be provided to managers and employees on all aspects of the system they are responsible for conducting
- Managers should document specific examples of effective and ineffective performance that explain the rationale for their ratings
- Organizational mechanisms should be in place for holding managers accountable for providing timely feedback
- Employees should be notified of deficiencies in a timely manner and provided with sufficient opportunity and feedback to improve in these areas
- Performance evaluations should be reviewed by a higher-level official or panel to ensure accurate ratings and promote the application of uniform standards across managers
- Employees should be allowed to provide input into their appraisal and to comment on the ratings or narrative provided by their managers
- If performance evaluations are used as a basis for deciding important outcomes, the decisions must align with the ratings given, for example, it would not be appropriate to terminate an employee who received high ratings in the absence of other documented information
- A formal appeals process should be included in the process that provides employees an opportunity to have their ratings reviewed and reconsidered at a higher level if they feel there are problems with them

In the legal arena, there are two concepts that are important to understand – adverse impact and validity – as they play a central role in determining the veracity of potential legal challenges an organization might face.

Adverse Impact

Adverse impact means that the outcomes from a human resources system can be associated with employees' race, gender, age, or other personal factors, such that individuals who belong to certain groups receive systematically less than individuals who belong to other groups. Potential adverse impact is evaluated against protected demographic groups, such as African Americans, Hispanics, females, and individuals over 40. There are different ways to examine adverse impact in a performance management system. If ratings are directly tied to outcomes such as pay increases, bonuses, or stock options, one can examine whether there are systematic and significant differences in the rewards received by different groups. A simple way to examine this involves use of the four-fifths rule.[2]

Example:
Calculation of Adverse Impact Using 4/5ths Rule

In a group of 75 males and 75 females, assume 45 females and 68 males receive a 10K bonus based on their performance ratings. Here are the calculations you would perform:

- The proportion of females receiving the bonus is 45/75 or 60%.
- The proportion of males receiving the bonus is 68/75 or 90%.
- The proportion of females receiving the bonus compared to males is 60%/90% or 67%.

Using this approach, adverse impact exists if the proportion of protected group members (females) receiving an outcome is less than four-fifths or 80% of the proportion of majority group members (males) receiving the same outcome. Because the proportion of females receiving a 10K bonus compared to males is only 67%, we would conclude that the performance management system is producing an adverse impact against females.

If a human resources system is shown to produce adverse impact and the organization wishes to continue using that system, there are legal requirements that the system must have demonstrated job relevance or validity. The existence of adverse impact without validity leaves the organization vulnerable to challenges against which it will not be able to prevail. While validity can be used as a defense for a performance management system that produces adverse impact, it is wise to minimize adverse impact to the extent possible. This not only decreases the chance that the organization will face costly and time-consuming legal challenges, but it also helps to avoid unfavorable views of an organization that can occur when its human resources systems are known to produce adverse impact.

Because adverse impact reflects the proportion of majority versus protected group members who receive desirable outcomes, it cannot be assessed until after the appraisal process is complete and final pay, promotion, etc. decisions have been made. This is obviously late in the game to realize that a system may be producing undesirable levels of adverse impact. For this reason, other analyses can be performed to evaluate the likelihood that a system will produce adverse impact. Specifically, one can examine the average performance rating scores that different groups receive using a statistic called the "Effect Size."[3]

Example:
Examination of Potential Adverse Impact Using "Effect Sizes"

Continuing with the example of 75 females and 75 males, we would:

- Calculate the average rating score for the group of 75 females
- Calculate average rating score for the group of 75 males
- Transform these average rating scores into a statistic that represents the difference in the average rating between the two groups. This statistic is commonly called the "effect size" or "group difference in standard deviation units"

Continued

Interpreting effect sizes:

- Effect sizes of 0 indicate no difference in the ratings given to the two groups
- Effect sizes of 1.00 or more indicate a very large difference in the average ratings given to the two groups
- Effect sizes that may seem small, in the .30 to .40 range, can produce considerable adverse impact in the outcomes received.
- There is not a specific effect size that is okay versus not okay – however, it is best to strive for effect sizes that are as small as possible.

Validity

If performance ratings are linked to important outcomes and produce an adverse impact against a protected group, the law requires that the system be shown to measure important requirements of the job, or in other words, be a content-valid system. Although there are other types of validity, content validity is the most practical and acceptable form of validity for performance management systems. Content validation requires conducting a thorough analysis to identify a job's critical performance requirements. Job requirements are the important work behaviors or tasks that are performed and the competencies that are required to effectively perform these work behaviors and tasks. The performance management system must focus on measuring how effectively employees perform critical work requirements. Content validity is demonstrated through a series of expert judgments, which document that the performance measures comprehensively assess important job requirements. A brief overview of the validation process is shown below, following steps 1–7, and more detailed guidance for developing valid outcome (i.e., results) and behavioral performance measures is provided in the next two chapters.

Good to Know:
Steps to Develop Content Valid Performance Measures

Step 1

Collect preliminary information about important job requirements (work behaviors, tasks, competencies) from reviewing job information, observing the job, or interviewing job experts.

↓

Step 2

Develop draft lists of work behaviors or tasks and the competencies required to perform these tasks.

↓

Step 3

Review and revise the list of work requirements with job experts (usually incumbents) that are diverse in terms of their demographics, locations in which work is performed, specific job functions, and any other factors that may impact the way the job is performed.

↓

Step 4

Survey a sufficiently large and representative sample of job incumbents or their supervisors, asking them to rate which job requirements are most critical for effective job performance.

↓

Step 5

Analyze the survey data to prioritize the most important job requirements (tasks, work behaviors, and competencies).

↓

Step 6

Develop rating standards for raters to use in evaluating performance on the most critical job requirements.

↓

Step 7

Conduct workshops with job experts to verify that the performance measures assess critical job requirements and that rating standards accurately describe the performance expectations for the job.

Chapter 7

Developing Objectives and Measuring Results

There are two primary activities involved in developing measures of results. The first is identifying performance objectives that state the outcomes an employee is expected to achieve. The second is specifying these in sufficient, measurable detail that it is clear to both managers and employees whether or not the objectives have been met. Ideally, the results to be achieved should be tied to the organization's strategy and goals. As discussed, this is typically achieved by developing cascading goals, where organizational goals are cascaded down through the different levels to individuals. These linkages help to ensure that the work of all organizational entities is aligned and focused on achieving important organizational goals. Although an individual's objectives should support higher level goals, an employee's development needs can also be taken into account in setting their objectives. These can be targeted to improving current job performance or preparing the employee for career advancement.

Linking Individual Objectives to Higher-Level Goals

There are two strategies that can be used when linking individual goals to higher level goals at the next level:

• Start with an employee's individual performance outcomes and work upward to link them to relevant higher-level goals

- Start with a higher-level goal that is relevant to an employee's job and work downward to develop an individual performance objective

The decision about whether to link upwards or downwards is a personal preference. Some find it easier to start with something concrete from their job and work upwards towards a less-tangible concept. Others find it easier to start with a broader, higher-level concept and develop something concrete they can do on their job that relates to this. An example of how department goals could be cascaded to individual objectives appears below. Note that the individual objectives are related to only one of the department goals. Objectives can be related to more than one goal at the next higher level, but it is unlikely that goals at one level will relate to all of the goals at the next level.

Example:
Individual Goals Cascaded from Department Goals Human Resources Department Goals

- Automate 60% of HR transactional processes by the end of year
- Create and staff a new Organizational Design and Change Management unit by end of year
- Develop a process to efficiently and cost effectively tie performance to rewards

Individual Objectives for Human Resources Professional

- Design and gain leadership approval for a new performance management system that links performance with pay by March
- Implement a Performance Management System by end of year with at least 90% of the employees receiving completed appraisals in first year and at least 80% of employees and managers indicating satisfaction with system based on survey results

Practical Exercise

At the end of this chapter, practical Training Exercise 6 can be used to help employees learn how to link individual objectives to higher-level objectives.

Identifying Individual Objectives

There are several guidelines that should be followed to develop effective performance objectives.[1] The first is that difficult but attainable objectives lead to more effective performance than moderately difficult goals. Second, in order for employees to achieve their objectives, they must feel committed to them and they must feel they are achievable. If employees feel that they cannot reach their objectives, they will be de-motivated to try. This is why it is important to ensure that employees accept their objectives and are motivated to achieve them. The best way to ensure this is to make employees an active part of the objective-setting process and work with them to arrive at objectives that are challenging and achievable. It is also important for managers to communicate and commit their support by providing guidance and resources to employees as well as removing obstacles to goal attainment. The "SMART" mnemonic helps managers and employees remember the key characteristics of effective objectives.

Tips:
SMART Guidelines for Establishing Effective Performance Objectives

- Specific: clearly stated and direct, defining the end results to be achieved
- Measurable: can be compared to a standard
- Attainable: difficult, achievable, and realistic, to motivate performance
- Relevant: have a direct and obvious link to organizational success factors or goals
- Timely: measured in deadlines, due dates, cycles or schedules

While the idea of setting individual objectives may seem straightforward, the process of doing this is usually more time-consuming and difficult than people expect. Especially initially, when managers and employees are not accustomed to developing objectives, they find it challenging to identify and clearly define them. One reason is that both managers and employees tend to naturally think in terms of the work behaviors employees perform on the job and not tangible, well-defined outcomes. For example, job descriptions typically contain

Example:
Translating Work Behaviors into Performance Objectives

Work Behavior	Objective
Manages delivery of custom-developed programs and projects for customers	Lead the XYZ project. Make sure all work is delivered according to the established milestone chart and project schedule, ending June 15. Effectively meet unit's needs for an improved staffing process as defined by receiving at least satisfactory scores and an average rating of "4" on a 5-point scale on all satisfaction indices assessed on the standard satisfaction survey.
Conducts studies to evaluate HR program effectiveness	Independently plan and conduct an evaluation study of the performance management process, including assessment of hard metrics (completion rates, analyses of ratings) and user satisfaction measures. Design methodology and research instruments and conduct data analyses according to professional standards for reliability and validity. By March 30, write report that requires no grammatical editing and minimal substantive editing. Technical report will include detailed and practical recommendations for improving the process.

work behaviors or job tasks. Identifying performance objectives requires going beyond these and thinking about the specific outcomes, products, or services that result from work activities. Two examples of work activities appear on the previous page, along with how these could be translated into performance objectives. The first work activity is to manage customer projects. An objective from this activity could be managing a specific project according to a project schedule and meeting customer satisfaction metrics in the end. The second work activity is to conduct evaluations of human resources programs. An objective of this activity might be to conduct a specific program evaluation study, where defined quality and timeliness metrics are met.

Ensuring Expected Results of Objectives are Measurable

Performance objectives should be clearly defined in terms of measurable outcomes so that both managers and employees know when and whether the objective has been achieved. Jobs that lend themselves best to setting measurable objectives have static performance requirements and hard productivity measures (e.g., dollar volume of sales, profitability, miles driven, or pieces produced). On the surface, writing objectives for these types of jobs may seem easy and straightforward. But, consider the following questions:

- Did the worker who produced the most pieces also produce the highest quality pieces?
- Did one employee have more modern equipment than another, enabling her to produce a higher volume of product, irrespective of how hard either worked?
- Was the driver who went the furthest distance speeding and endangering others the entire way?
- Was one salesperson's territory in Wyoming and another's in New York City? Based on the number and proximity of potential customers, the person in New York may have had more opportunity to make sales than the person in Wyoming.

The bottom line is that even when measures seem straightforward to define, it is important to think through the consequences of those that are selected. For example, quantity measures are usually easier to define than quality measures. However, if only quantity metrics are used, employees will focus on producing a lot, possibly to the detriment of producing quality. Likewise, it's important to take into account the individual's opportunity to perform in his or her particular circumstances. If one employee is working on a machine that produces products twice as fast as another employee's

---

Tips:
How to Measure the Results of Objectives

Timeliness: Timeframe in which work is performed

- Responded to requests for information within 24 hours
- Provided financial reports summarizing program operations on a quarterly basis

Quality: How well work is performed

- Improved the layout for navigating a website to make it more user-friendly and easier to use as indicated by 20% improvement in user survey satisfaction results
- Independently created a report containing relevant and concise information on program operations that required no revisions
- Developed an online training program for employees where trainees successfully learned 85% of the material

Quantity: How much work is performed

- Responded to 95% of requests
- Provided computer training to 90% of employees
- Conducted two on-site reviews each month to assess compliance with regulations

Financial metrics: Efficient use of funds, revenues, profits, savings

- Budgeted operations to achieve a 10% cost savings compared to last year
- Convinced customer to increase expenditures for services by 15% more than last year

machine, the employee with the slower machine will never be able to outperform the one with the faster machine, no matter how hard that employee works. Rather than impose the same goals on all staff, consideration should be given to real differences in opportunities employees may have so that stretch but achievable objectives can be set for everyone. There are four types of measures that are commonly used: timeliness, quality, quantity, and financial metrics.

Although there are four primary ways to measure results, these can be used together. In fact, linking different types of measures usually improves the quality of the measure, for example:

- Processed 99% of candidate job applications within one week of receiving them (quantity and timeliness).
- Developed an online training course that taught 90% employees how to independently use automated transactional systems and reduced training costs by $500/employee (quantity, quality, and financial metrics).

The more detail managers can provide in terms of the target objective and expected results, the more clearly the performance expectations will be understood. In addition, this will also help avoid disagreements about whether an objective has been successfully met. A very important caveat, however, is not to fall prey to measuring peripheral aspects of the objective that may be easy to measure but do not assess the most important things. For example, meeting a deadline is easy to measure but improving customer service may be what's important to measure.

While many different types of measures can be identified, there is the very practical issue of which and how many of these can be reliably and accurately assessed without creating systems and processes that are so burdensome that they die of their own weight. To implement and maintain an objective setting process that is effective and manageable over time, the measures selected need to capture what's most important, reflect critical bottom line results, and be practical to obtain. Shown below are several examples of objectives that are more or less well defined. These examples show how a clear definition of expected results can increase understanding and avoid disagreement around whether or not objectives were actually met.

Example:
Performance Objectives

Well-defined Performance Objectives

- By June 15, prepare a document that requires no grammatical editing and minimal substantive editing containing a methodology and focus group questions to further understand and evaluate responses to the annual employee satisfaction survey.
- Reduce by 10% the amount of time needed to process 33,000 hiring requisitions.
- Provide responses to requests for benefits information and human resources procedures within 48 hours of receipt.
- Develop a web-based tutorial program to assist employees in proper implementation of the organization's new performance management process by April 15.
- Draft and submit to the Human Resources Vice President a plan and timeline that is accepted without revision for implementing a new automated process to track employee development activities and formal training.
- Implement a new automated benefits administration process by July 15 and achieve user satisfaction indices of at least 95%.
- Provide 100% accurate financial reports summarizing benefits expenses on a quarterly basis.

Poorly Defined Performance Objectives

- Collaborate with Human Resources team members to ensure regulatory requirements are met.
- Provide effective customer service.
- Monitor the progress of Human Resources program operations.
- Perform activities of limited scope and complexity in the application of Human Resources regulations and procedures.
- Collaborate as appropriate with other organizations and their representatives on specific projects.
- Communicate effectively, both verbally and in writing, to relate findings, identify problems, and draft recommendations clearly and accurately.

In developing objectives, managers need to ensure that they are written to reflect fully successful performance for the job and level, such that most employees would receive "meets expectations" ratings on their objectives. If an employee exceeds the objectives (for example, produces significantly better quality, quantity, timeliness, or impact than defined), he or she should be given a higher rating. However, high ratings on performance objectives should be reserved for individuals who perform well beyond the expectations for their job, and these ratings should be the exception rather than the rule.

Practical Exercise

At the end of this chapter, practical Training Exercise 7 can be used to help teach managers and employees how to identify effective individual objectives.

Overcoming Challenges in Using Individual Objectives for Performance Management

There are several challenges associated with using individual objectives as the basis for performance management.[2]

Inconsistency among managers can result in objectives that are too easy, unattainable, or unsystematic across individuals who occupy the same job.[3,4] If managers are not trained to set objectives of similar difficulty and complexity for employees in the same job, one employee's objective could be to perform a simple data collection task, while another's in the same job could be to manage the design and implementation of a complex program evaluation process. If the overall impact and contribution of the results associated with these different objectives are not considered, the employee who executed a simple data collection task could be considered as performing equivalently to the employee who implemented a complex program evaluation process, simply because they both achieved their objectives. Thus, a key challenge is ensuring that fair, equitable, and job relevant objectives are set for all employees.

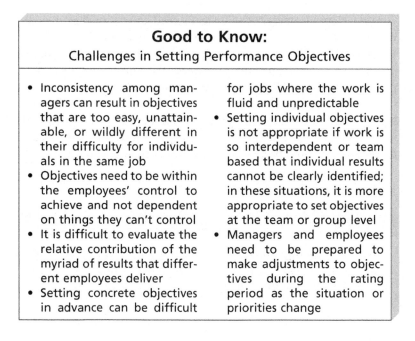

Good to Know:

Challenges in Setting Performance Objectives

- Inconsistency among managers can result in objectives that are too easy, unattainable, or wildly different in their difficulty for individuals in the same job
- Objectives need to be within the employees' control to achieve and not dependent on things they can't control
- It is difficult to evaluate the relative contribution of the myriad of results that different employees deliver
- Setting concrete objectives in advance can be difficult

for jobs where the work is fluid and unpredictable
- Setting individual objectives is not appropriate if work is so interdependent or team based that individual results cannot be clearly identified; in these situations, it is more appropriate to set objectives at the team or group level
- Managers and employees need to be prepared to make adjustments to objectives during the rating period as the situation or priorities change

In highly routine and predictable jobs, it is sometimes possible to predefine a set of objectives that apply uniformly to all employees. This not only saves time that would otherwise be spent by each manager and staff member developing individual objectives, but it also ensures that all employees in the same job are held accountable for the same expectations and standards. When identical objectives apply to everyone in a job, job analysis procedures like those discussed in Chapter 6 can be used to define these, ensuring their job relevance.

In many jobs, the objectives for different employees vary significantly, depending on the nature of the individual's duties and assignments. When it is not possible to use the same objectives for all employees, it is best to have supervisors develop individual objectives from validated tasks or work behaviors that have been identified for the job. The objectives will need to contain more specific information than the tasks or work behaviors (e.g., what specific project, customer, product, etc. the employee is responsible for), as well as specific quality, quantity, and timeliness expectations. However, by starting with a list of validated tasks or work behaviors, the objectives developed for each employee can be linked to valid job content. As objectives are defined for employees holding similar or identical jobs, they can be compiled and reviewed across managers. This helps to ensure that similarly difficult and complex objectives are being set for individuals in the same job and level.

Case Scenario:
Leveraging Objectives

After objectives were written for individuals occupying each job in a political organization, they were catalogued and stored in a database. This made it possible for managers and employees to search the database for objectives that might be relevant to different employees' jobs. They were then able to use the already developed objectives as a starting point and edit them to be customized for other employees. Over time, this resulted in increasing levels of consistency in the objectives that were developed for employees in similar jobs.

Even if training and examples are provided to help managers develop objectives, they will still be at least somewhat unique to each employee, in most cases. An issue then becomes how to evaluate the relative contribution of the myriad of results that different employees deliver. Given that some employees deliver higher impact results than others, it would not be fair to consider all employees who achieve their objectives as performing the same. An effective strategy that has been used in several public and private sector organizations to address this issue is to develop standards for evaluating the relative contribution of different results, in addition to evaluating whether or not timeliness, quality, quantity, or financial measures were achieved. The use of individual performance objectives without this additional evaluation fails to differentiate between employees who are contributing more or less and for differentially rewarding them.[5] An example of such standards is shown next.

Example: Performance Standards for Evaluating Overall Contribution of Results		
Low Impact	**Moderate Impact**	**High Impact**
Result was straightforward to accomplish and had a small impact on business results.	Result had a positive impact on efficiency or effectiveness of operations.	Result had an extremely positive impact, producing significant cost reductions or profit increases.

Another challenge is that setting concrete objectives in advance can be difficult for jobs that are unpredictable or constantly changing.[6,7] Consider the challenges in trying to develop specific objectives for R&D jobs where it is impossible to predict when meaningful discoveries will occur. An effective strategy for these types of jobs is to set shorter-term objectives that are more predictable. Feedback can be given and interim appraisals conducted as employees reach key milestones during the rating period. In fact, given the fluid nature of many work environments, some experts have advocated not even trying to set longer-term objectives, claiming that this is an exercise in futility, and instead recommended that the focus be on setting shorter-term objectives as the work evolves.

A final challenge in setting objectives occurs when it is difficult to associate outcomes with a specific person's effort, because the work is team-focused or requires significant interdependence with others. In these circumstances, objectives should be set at the level where the key work products are produced. If jobs are so intertwined or dependent on a team, it may not be practical or appropriate to set individual objectives. Instead, objectives should be set at the higher group or team level.

Case Scenario:
Setting Achievable Objectives in Changing Situations

In an international lending organization, objectives were initially set for the entire year in spite of the fact that the work was extremely fluid and unpredictable. Evaluation of the performance management system after two years showed that the system documentation was filled with explanations for why objectives did not get accomplished as planned, rather than filled with what had been accomplished. Employees and managers were also frustrated by the fact that their performance management system was filled with excuses for why goals were not achieved. This organization successfully improved its performance management process and user satisfaction with the process by moving to shorter-term, more predictable objectives.

Setting Objectives Collaboratively with Staff

The first performance conversation managers and employees should have at the beginning of the rating cycle is to identify the employee's performance objectives. Both managers and employees need to do some advance planning for this discussion. The meeting should take place in private without interruption. It's important that the meeting is a collaborative effort where employees participate and provide their input, so they will be committed to their goals. During the meeting, managers should discuss the department or office goals with employees and their ideas about the objectives the employee should achieve. Depending on the level of the employees and the type of work they are doing, it may be appropriate for employees to also discuss objectives they wish to achieve. During this conversation, there are several common questions that typically arise, which managers need to be prepared to address.

No more than three to five major objectives should be identified for each employee. Major objectives refer to key deliverables and significant projects or outcomes employees are expected to achieve. While it is frequently possible to set sub-goals for major objectives and employees may wish to do this for their own planning purposes, it is not recommended that the objectives included in an employee's

Tips:
How to Address Frequently Asked Questions about Setting Objectives

How does my job description relate to my objectives?

- Job descriptions include work behaviors and tasks
- Objectives focus on products, services, and accomplishments that result from work behaviors/tasks
- You need to go beyond work behaviors to define measurable objectives

I think my objectives are too easy, too difficult, or not what I thought I would be working on.

- Identify the employee's specific concerns
- Make a decision about whether or not to revise the objectives

If something unforeseen prevents me from achieving my objectives, will I still be accountable?

- One of employees' responsibilities is to keep managers informed of any issues that interfere with accomplishing their objectives
- Objectives may need to be modified to account for these things

To achieve my objectives, I have to rely on other people. If they don't come through, how will I be affected?

- Employees should first discuss their needs with involved others and keep lines of communication open with them
- Employees also need to keep managers informed of issues that impact achieving their objectives

Do I have to wait until my final review session to find out if I am achieving my objectives in a satisfactory manner?

- Managers need to provide on-going feedback about how employees are performing throughout the rating period
- Employees should seek feedback from managers at any time they wish

performance plan contain this level of detail. Having a large number of narrow objectives at very specific levels of detail will be cumbersome to manage and therefore are not recommended.

Once managers and employees have come to agreement on the employee's objectives, a strategy that can facilitate employee ownership is to have employees prepare the wording of their objectives for their performance plans. Managers can then review and sign off on the final set of objectives. This not only helps to ensure mutual understanding of what is expected but also makes efficient use of managers' time in executing the process with many direct reports.

During the rating period, managers and staff may need to revisit the objectives as unforeseen events occur that interfere with achieving them. Although objectives can be changed during the rating period, it is best to "freeze" them at least three months prior to when ratings will be made. A key concern in implementing a performance management system is ensuring that employees understand their expectations and are provided with sufficient time to achieve them. Last minute changes can lead to perceptions of "changing the rules at the 11th hour" and may lead employees to challenge their evaluations.

The Bottom Line

The development of individual performance objectives that drive key results can be an important and effective component of a performance management process. However, developing fair, job-relevant, and useful objectives requires training and considerable effort on the part of managers, employees, and human resources staff. If organizational members are not committed to developing effective objectives and doing this consistently for all employees, individual objectives should not be included in the performance management process. Poorly developed objectives will not only be de-motivating to staff but can leave an organization vulnerable to potentially successful legal challenges. Thus, if there is unwillingness to devote the time, energy, and resources necessary to overcome the inherent challenges involved in developing good objectives and monitoring the effectiveness and completion of these, the best alternative is to include only behavioral performance standards in the system. The development of these is discussed next.

Practical Exercises

Exercise 6:
Linking Objectives to Higher Level Objectives

Trainer Note. This exercise helps trainees write performance objectives, based on work behaviors, and link them to higher-level goals. It can be conducted individually or in small groups. The work behaviors provided below are examples and should be customized to the organization in which training is provided. Also, objectives for the relevant office, division, etc. will need to be provided as part of the exercise. Following completion of the exercises, participants can report on some of the objectives they wrote and the linkages they made.

Writing and Linking Performance Objectives to Higher-Level Outcomes

Below are four work behaviors that apply to several jobs within XYZ organization. Choose *any two* of these and do two things:

- Write an individual performance outcome that reflects the work behavior.
- Link the performance outcome to a related office, division, and organizational objective.

Work Behavior 1. Analyzes and evaluates the effectiveness of program operations in meeting the established goals and objectives of the group.	
Individual Outcome	
Office Objective	
Division Objective	
Organizational Objective	

Work Behavior 2. Ensures that all grant applications comply with applicable program announcements.	
Individual Outcome	
Office Objective	
Division Objective	
Organizational Objective	

Work Behavior 3. Provides technical advice and assistance on designated program operations to ensure compliance with office requirements.	
Individual Outcome	
Office Objective	
Division Objective	
Organizational Objective	

Work Behavior 4. Provides assistance in developing strategies and implementing plans for special projects or initiatives related to program operations.	
Individual Outcome	
Office Objective	
Division Objective	
Organizational Objective	

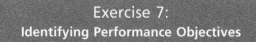

Exercise 7:
Identifying Performance Objectives

Trainer Note. This exercise helps trainees distinguish between performance objectives and work behaviors. Note that "X"s have been included on the form, denoting those items that reflect better defined performance objectives. Following independent completion of the exercise below, review participants' responses and facilitate a discussion about how the unmarked items could be further defined to make them more effective performance objectives. The items in this exercise can be tailored to be more relevant to the organization/jobs for which training is provided.

Identifying Effective Performance Objectives

This exercise will help you distinguish between performance objectives and work behaviors. Below is a list of 12 statements. Some are appropriately phrased as performance results and others are not. Place an "X" in the space next to those statements that you believe are written as performance results.

1. X Develop a comprehensive plan, questions, and a written protocol for conducting a series of focus groups to evaluate customer perceptions of the new "KEYMAX" product line by June 15.

2. Review product sales information to determine if it complies with internal reporting requirements.

3. Communicate effectively, both verbally and in writing, to relate findings, identify problems, and draft recommendations clearly and accurately.

4. X Reduce by 10% the amount of time needed to process requisitions.

5. X Provide responses that fully satisfy customers' requests for technical support assistance within 48 hours of receipt.

6. **X** By March 15, develop a comprehensive training program where managers correctly learn 90% of the training content for how to conduct a panel interview process that will be used to make staffing decisions; by August 30, complete training and assess learning for all managerial staff.

7. Perform developmental activities of moderate scope and complexity to learn the proper application of regulations and procedures.

8. Monitor the progress of business operations.

9. **X** Prepare a written summary of what was observed during the ABC customer satisfaction focus group within one month of completion, including conclusions and recommendations for product improvement.

10. Provide effective customer service, planning, and evaluating to include providing responsive, timely, and effective service to customers and ensuring that their needs are fully met.

11. **X** Process purchase orders and reimbursements for travel expenses within one week of receipt.

12. Collaborate with other team members to ensure fiscal and regulatory requirements are met.

Chapter 8

Developing Behavioral Performance Standards

A popular trend for about the past twenty years has been for organizations to adopt competency models as a basis for their performance management and other human resources systems.[1] One advantage of competency models is that they communicate what is important to the organization's leadership and drive performance in desired areas. For example, if an organizational goal is to improve customer service, then including a Customer Service competency not only communicates that this is a critical success factor but also focuses attention and rewards on this aspect of performance. Competency models usually include a comprehensive array of factors associated with success – technical, leadership, interpersonal, and personal.

While competency models have been enormously popular and adopted by many organizations, there has been debate and lack of clear definition about what a competency is:

- Ability factor?
- Skill factor?
- Knowledge factor?
- Personality factor?
- Performance factor?
- All of the above?

Here, competencies are defined as the knowledge, skills, abilities, and other personal characteristics that are most instrumental for achieving important job outcomes and contributing to organizational success.

Example:
Different Types of Competencies

- **Action Oriented.** Pursues work with energy, drive, and a strong accomplishment orientation.
- **Adaptability.** Works effectively and demonstrates flexibility in dealing with tough situations involving change, ambiguity, and stress.
- **Planning Work.** Efficiently develops and implements plans to accomplish goals.
- **Building and Construction.** Using materials, methods, and tools involved in the construction or repair of houses, buildings, or other structures.
- **Human Resources.** Applies principles and procedures for recruitment, staffing, training, compensation, benefits, labor relations, and personnel information systems.
- **Managing Systems and Processes.** Effectively uses systems and processes to measure, monitor, manage, or impact performance.
- **Customer Focus.** Investigates and takes action to meet customers' current and future needs.
- **Building Team Spirit.** Develops and maintains productive, effective, and high morale.
- **Strategic Leadership.** Creates a shared purpose, vision, or direction for the group or organization and inspires other to work toward it.

Many organizations have used fairly informal processes to develop their competencies, such as interviewing organizational leaders or convening focus groups to discuss important success factors, rather than using rigorous job analytic approaches such as those described in Chapter 6. If competency measures are used primarily for development, using informal processes to develop them is unlikely to yield significant negative consequences. However, if competency measures are used as the basis for human resources decisions, more formal and rigorous procedures for demonstrating their job-relevance are prudent to employ. A suggested approach for doing this is outlined following discussion of two important questions that first need to be addressed:

- How many competencies should be developed?
- Should highly job-specific or more generic performance standards be developed for different jobs?

How Many Competencies?

One advantage that competency models offer is that they provide a foundation for developing integrated human resources systems, such as staffing, training, promotion, succession planning, and performance management systems. However, the number and specificity of the competencies needed depend on their intended use, for example:

- To make entry-level staffing decisions, broad ability and personality competencies are typically developed and assessed, such as critical thinking, conscientiousness, and interpersonal skills
- If the purpose is staffing for a job that requires highly specialized skills, more specific technical competencies need to be identified and measured
- For training and career development, competencies need to include more general capabilities (communication skills, planning skills) as well as specialized technical knowledge and skills
- For performance management purposes, higher-level competencies are typically used that reflect the major performance requirements of a job Organizations usually identify between five and 12 higher-level competencies that are linked to their strategic objectives and critical success factors

While novice developers of performance management systems are sometimes tempted to include a large number of very specific competencies in their systems, rating and providing feedback on a large number of competencies take a considerable amount of time. Systems that contain too many competencies are not viewed positively or as practical by managers with many direct reports to evaluate. In addition, the number of competencies selected for performance management purposes is much less important than ensuring that those selected are well defined and reflect the most critical aspects of the job.

> ## Case Scenario:
> ### Fewer Competencies Can be Better
>
> Although the number of competencies used for performance management is typically between five and 12, an R&D organization decided to use only three – Technical Proficiency, Business Development, and Citizenship. The rationale was that they wanted the performance management system to be maximally efficient and manageable so that both managers and employees would be highly motivated to use it. They also wanted very clear and crisp definitions of the most critical factors that really made a difference. They felt this could best be accomplished with a very small number of competencies that were precisely defined and reflected the most essential performance requirements. Users reported high satisfaction with the performance management process and that it helped them focus on the most critical aspects of their jobs.

The challenge in developing competency models to serve multiple purposes concerns the need for job information that is both specific and general. A way to address this challenge is to create hierarchical

> ## Example:
> ### Lower Level Competencies for "Communicating with Others" Competency
>
> - Speaking – Expresses information to individuals or groups taking into account the audience and the nature of the information to be presented.
> - Listening – Receives, attends to, interprets, understands, and responds to verbal messages or other cues, picking out and understanding important information.
> - Persuasion/Influence – Persuasively presents thoughts and ideas, gaining commitment and ensuring support for proposed ideas.
> - Developing Materials – Prepares documents that communicate information in an organized, logical, and coherent manner, with supporting information and examples.
> - Writing Mechanics – Uses standard syntax and sentence structure, and correct spelling, punctuation, and grammar.

competency models, where more detailed competencies are categorized under more general competencies.[2] Lower-level competencies that relate to the "Communicating with Others" competency appear in the example. The advantage of this approach is that more specific competencies are portrayed as interrelated instances of broader competencies within the context of a job. This provides an organized, understandable foundation of detailed information that is needed for staffing and training of specialized competencies, while also providing higher-level competencies that are more practical for performance management purposes.

How Customized Should Performance Standards Be?

For performance management purposes, experienced practitioners agree that competencies should be defined in terms of performance standards that help managers differentiate between employees who are performing more or less effectively than others. However, decisions need to be made about how many different sets of performance standards should be developed and how customized these should be. There is no one best approach, as there are advantages and disadvantages to different options. There are three key decisions that need to be made:

- *How much customization for different jobs?* – Will performance standards be developed that can be applied across all jobs or will they be customized to reflect the specific content of individual jobs?
- *How many effectiveness levels?* – Within each competency, how many levels of performance effectiveness will be defined and what will these be (e.g., below expectations, meets expectations, exceeds expectations)?
- *How many experience levels?* – Will one set of performance standards be developed that applies across all experience levels or should separate standards be developed for different levels of work (e.g., entry-level, full performance, expert)?

How Much Customization for Different Jobs?

Sometimes fairly general performance standards are developed for each competency that can be used across all of the jobs within an organization. In this scenario, technical aspects of the job are often handled by having a "Technical Proficiency" competency, also defined in a general manner that is applicable across jobs.

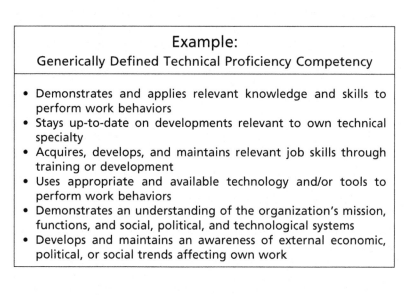

Example:
Generically Defined Technical Proficiency Competency

- Demonstrates and applies relevant knowledge and skills to perform work behaviors
- Stays up-to-date on developments relevant to own technical specialty
- Acquires, develops, and maintains relevant job skills through training or development
- Uses appropriate and available technology and/or tools to perform work behaviors
- Demonstrates an understanding of the organization's mission, functions, and social, political, and technological systems
- Develops and maintains an awareness of external economic, political, or social trends affecting own work

An alternative to using common standards that apply across jobs is to customize the competencies to some degree to reflect the specific requirements of individual jobs. Several examples of how this has been done appear below.

If common competencies and more general standards are used that apply across all jobs, a potential downside is that some organizational members may have difficulty seeing their specific jobs in the standards, and they may react less favorably to these than more customized standards. As a result, managers may need to translate more generally written standards into more specific expectations for a given employee's job. On the other hand, a practical advantage of using common standards across jobs is that the development time and resources are significantly less than what is needed to develop customized competencies and performance standards for different jobs. Using common standards across jobs also results in communicating more consistent expectations to organizational members, which can be important if one goal of the competency model is to

Case Scenarios:
Different Options for
Competency Customization

- In an *auditing organization*, a common set of competency names was used across jobs, but three different sets of customized performance standards were used to define different expectations for three different types of jobs – professional, administrative, and managerial.
- In an *information technology organization*, common performance standards were used to define a set of core competencies (interpersonal effectiveness, teamwork, communication) that applied across all jobs. However, customized technical competencies and performance standards were developed for each specific job.
- In a *Federal Government law enforcement organization*, customized competencies and performance standards were developed for each of 22 job families, including Special Agent, Human Resources, Information Technology, Engineering, Acquisitions, Finance, Management, and others.

drive performance in certain strategic areas. The decision about how much to customize the competencies and performance standards depends on three things:

- The goals the organization is trying to achieve with its performance management system
- The resources available for developing and maintaining the system
- What will be viewed as acceptable and effective to organizational members

How Many Effectiveness Levels?

To anchor managers' judgments of performance, it is important to define standards for different levels of effectiveness within each competency.

Example:
Performance Effectiveness Levels

- Significantly Below Expectations
- Meets Minimal Expectations Only
- Meets Expectations Fully
- Exceeds Expectations
- Significantly Exceeds Expectations

Obviously, performance standards could be defined for more or fewer effectiveness levels. Typically, at least two sets of performance standards, describing what it takes to "Meet" and "Exceed" expectations are defined. Sometimes, standards are also written for minimal or below expectations performance. It is rare, however, to see performance standards written for more than three effectiveness levels. The reason is because any standards written need to clearly and unambiguously describe the performance expectations at each level of effectiveness. When one attempts to write standards for too many different effectiveness levels, the descriptions start melding together and it is difficult to see clear and unambiguous distinctions between them. When there are not clear distinctions between the standards for different effectiveness levels, managers have difficulty systematically applying them as well as explaining to employees the rationale for one rating versus another. For this reason, it is recommended that performance standards be defined for no more than three effectiveness levels.

If performance information will be used for decision-making, a numerical rating scale should be used in conjunction with the performance standards. A five- or seven-point scale is used most often because it provides a sufficient number of rating points to differentiate between employees in terms of their performance. A rating scale of less than five points does not usually provide adequate differentiation among employees, while a rating scale of more than seven points adds complexity without significantly more differentiation. With a five-point scale, three ratings are commonly used, from 3 (meets expectations) to 5 (exceeds expectations). With a seven-point scale, four ratings are commonly used, from 4 (meets expectations) to 7 (exceeds

Case Scenario:
A Good Idea for Writing Effectiveness Standards

An idea developed in a protective service organization was to create standards that focus only on what is different between the meets and exceeds expectations levels, rather than provide full descriptions of effectiveness at each level. These standards were coined "delta scales" because of their focus on what is different between the effectiveness levels. To receive an "Exceeds Expectations" rating, an employee needed to do everything described at the "Meets Expectations" level as well as the *additional requirements* defining the "Exceeds Expectations" level. Users reported high satisfaction using these standards. They found it helpful to have the differences between the effectiveness levels pinpointed rather than having to read through lengthy descriptions and dig for the differences.

expectations). The choice of whether to use a five- or seven-point scale is personal preference.

Those who prefer a five-point scale say . . .
- More than five rating points is too many, and it's not possible to make such fine-grained performance distinctions.
- They want to keep the performance management system as simple as possible, and a seven-point scale is overly complex.

Those who prefer a seven-point scale say . . .
- The availability of seven rating points is important to spread out the ratings as much as possible, especially given managers' tendencies to use the higher rating points.

Irrespective of the number of rating scale points, the relationship between these and the performance standards needs to be clearly articulated so that raters can apply them in a uniform and fair manner. Ratings based on numerical scales can easily be averaged or summed across competencies to derive a summary score for decision-making.

> ## Example:
> ### Five-Point and Seven-Point Scales with Defined Rating Points
>
> | | |
> |---|---|
> | 5 = Almost always performs like the "Exceeds Expectations" standards
4 = Sometimes performs like the "Exceeds Expectations" standards and sometimes performs like the "Meets Expectations" standards
3 = Almost always performs like the "Meets Expectations" standards
2 = Sometimes performs like the "Meets Expectations" standards and sometimes performs like the "Below Expectations" standards
1 = Almost always performs like the "Below Expectations" standards | 7 = Almost always performs like the "Exceeds Expectations" standards
6 = Usually performs like the "Exceeds Expectations" standards but sometimes performs like the "Meets Expectations" standards
5 = Usually performs like the "Meets Expectations" standards but sometimes performs like the "Exceeds Expectations" standards
4 = Almost always performs like the "Meets Expectations" standards
3 = Usually performs like the "Meets Expectations" standards but sometimes performs like the "Below Expectations" standards
2 = Usually performs like the "Below Expectations" standards but sometimes performs like "Meets Expectations" standards
1 = Almost always performs like the "Below Expectations" standards |

How Many Job Levels?

While organizations can choose to define more or less customized standards for different types of jobs, it is not recommended that the same standards be used for different job levels. Because employees at different job levels are paid differently, based on their knowledge, responsibility, and contributions, performance standards need to reflect the different levels of complexity, difficulty, and independence that characterize these.

Example:
Job Levels

- *Entry-level employee.* Requires supervision and guidance to learn work; performs simple, straightforward tasks.
- *Full performance (or journeyman) level employee.* Has acquired the full range of skills to perform moderately complex work independently.
- *Expert employee.* Has developed deep expertise through experience to perform the most complex and difficult assignments; provides technical guidance to others.
- *Supervisor.* Serves a formal first-line supervisor of a team or unit.
- *Manager.* Serves a manager of multiple teams or units.

Similar to the discussion above regarding definition of different effectiveness levels, standards for different job levels need to clearly and unambiguously describe the performance expectations at each level. For progression purposes, it is also important to clearly articulate how the performance expectations change as one moves through different job levels. Thus, the standards for different experience levels should focus on:

- Differences in the tasks and activities performed at different levels
- Differences in the complexity of the work at different levels
- Differences in the amount of supervision at different levels
- Any other concrete factor that describes how the work is changes at the different levels

The differences between job levels should not simply be about doing the same work more or less effectively. Finally, it is not sufficient to say that work is "complex" at one level and "highly complex" at the next level, because everyone will have different interpretations of what this means. Rather, it is important to describe what makes the work more complex from one level to the next.

One caveat in writing standards for different job levels is that there may not be different expectations for each and every competency.

Case Scenario:
Complexity Differences that Define Different Experience Levels

In a technology development organization, planning activities were defined for three levels of experience along a complexity continuum:

- At level 1, employees assist in planning small, straightforward portions of projects under the supervision of a senior staff member.
- At level 2, employees independently plan small, straightforward projects where there are no requirements to coordinate with others.
- At level 3, employees independently plan large, complex projects that require coordinating with multiple other units or organizations; handling logistics that involve multiple facilities, people, and equipment; and managing million dollar-plus project budgets.

Certainly, there should be differences for many, if not most, of the competencies showing the higher level responsibilities that accompany higher-level salaries and expectations at different job levels. However, for things like integrity, initiative and motivation, and security consciousness, the same high standards are usually expected, irrespective of the job level.

It is important to think through how many job levels should be defined. If one attempts to write behavioral standards for too many levels, the descriptions start overlapping and it is difficult to see clear distinctions between them. Many organizations have a large number of job levels, sometimes as many as 15 or more, where there are overlapping requirements and unclear distinctions between them. Not only are systems with this many levels difficult to manage efficiently, but it is extremely difficult to articulate clear performance standards for this many levels, as well as multiple effectiveness levels within them. Prior to developing a new performance management system, it may be necessary to define fewer job levels so that the performance requirements for these levels are distinct and clear. Typically, anywhere from three job levels (entry-level, full performance, and manager) to a maximum of six levels (entry-level, full performance, expert, team leader, supervisor, and manager) are defined.

As a practical matter, careful consideration needs to be given to the implications of the decisions regarding the number of performance standards to be developed. For example, if one chooses to define six job levels with three performance effectiveness levels for 12 competencies that are customized for 20 separate jobs, over 4,000 unique performance standards would need to be written. The resources and time it would take to accomplish this may be prohibitive, in which case it would be practical to use more general standards that can be applied across jobs. Performance standards that can be applied across jobs for three effectiveness levels and three experience levels are shown in the examples below.

Example:
Standards for Entry-Level: Planning Work Competency

Below Expectations	Meets Expectations	Exceeds Expectations
Even with guidance, fails to prioritize and plan own work in a manner that ensures timely completion of work and proper coordination of activities with others.	With guidance and as directed, prioritizes, schedules, and plans own work activities to ensure tasks are completed in a timely manner. With guidance, coordinates project activities with co-workers and work unit and keeps others informed of progress on tasks.	**"Meets Expectations" plus does the following:** Takes initiative and demonstrates skill in organizing and planning work, resulting in efficiency and effectiveness far beyond what is ordinarily expected at this level. Anticipates potential issues or problems and takes action to prevent or mitigate their effects, resulting in an enhanced ability of the unit to accomplish its goals and objectives.

Example:
Standards for Full Performance or Journeyman Level: Planning Work Competency

Below Expectations	Meets Expectations	Exceeds Expectations
Fails to prioritize work for self or others to ensure timely completion of projects and assignments. Does not anticipate or take steps to mitigate obstacles that impact work schedule or delivery.	Independently prioritizes, plans, organizes, and schedules own work activities to ensure assignments are completed in a timely manner. Coordinates work activities with co-workers and work unit; takes initiative to keep others informed of progress, problems, or changes. Sees obvious problems and makes recommendations to overcome them so that progress is not impeded.	"Meets Expectations" plus does the following: Demonstrates a high level of skill in complex planning to include coordination across organizational units, multiple facilities, and solving thorny logistical problems, resulting in contributions far beyond what is expected at this level. Takes initiative to help others plan efforts for the group to ensure goals are met. Anticipates important roadblocks and takes effective preemptive action to prevent them, ensuring progress on projects.

Example: Performance Standards for Manager Level: Planning Work Competency		
Below Expectations	**Meets Expectations**	**Exceeds Expectations**
Fails to assign priorities or ineffectively prioritizes work for the group to ensure multiple, competing work demands are addressed. Does not anticipate or develop strategies to address obstacles facing the group.	Efficiently prioritizes, plans, organizes, and schedules projects and assignments to accomplish unit objectives, even under tight deadlines or in the face of unexpected events or numerous competing priorities. Effectively identifies and appropriately involves the right people in work activities, ensuring that they are well informed of progress, problems, and changes in work activities. Anticipates problems and roadblocks and effectively adjusts plans and schedules to overcome them, minimizing negative impact on the accomplishment of unit objectives.	**"Meets Expectations" plus does the following:** Demonstrates the highest levels of skill in prioritizing and overseeing the planning, organizing, and scheduling of numerous projects, resulting in maximum efficiency, accomplishment of very significant and difficult goals, and extremely high levels of productivity for the group. Anticipates even unique or subtle potential problems and roadblocks; proactively develops contingency plans to prevent or address potential problems; actively leverages lessons learned to help others avoid problems and thereby ensures effective progress and delivery of results.

An Efficient Approach to Developing Competencies and Performance Standards

Job analysis techniques, such as job observations, interviews, focus groups, and surveys are an effective means for identifying key competencies. To demonstrate that a performance measure is job-relevant or content valid, as discussed in Chapter 6, it is necessary to show that it assesses performance on work behaviors that are important for performing the job. While there are several approaches for developing valid competency models,[3] an effective and efficient process for defining content valid competencies and performance standards consists of three steps:

- Step 1: Develop Competencies Defined by Important Work Behaviors
- Step 2: Validate Competencies
- Step 3: Develop and Validate Performance Standards

Step 1: Develop Competencies Defined by Important Work Behaviors

The first step is to become familiar with the target job(s) by reviewing organizational and occupation-related documentation and talking with senior management for its perspective about the key competencies that are required for success. In this first step, decisions will need to be made about the general number of competencies to develop and whether common competencies and performance standards will be developed to apply to all jobs or be customized for different jobs. Decisions will also need to be made about how many experience levels and effectiveness levels to define. For purposes of illustrating the approach, assume the decision has been made to develop:

- Eight competencies and performance standards that will be applied across all jobs
- Two levels of effectiveness (meets expectations and exceeds expectation) for each of three experience levels (entry level, full performance level, and first-level manager).

Although these are the goals, the development and data collection processes discussed next will determine whether these goals are possible. For example, it may be that the exact same competencies and performance standards are not relevant (or valid) for all jobs.

Based on information collected from the organization's leadership and the review of job materials, a preliminary set of competencies is identified and a general definition is written for each. Each competency is then further defined by approximately five to eight work behaviors. Articulating how the competencies are manifested in observable work behaviors is important for establishing the job-relevance of the model. While the number of work behaviors used to define a competency can vary, five to eight is recommended for this approach. Work behaviors are written at a higher level of generality than task statements so that they will apply across jobs rather than be highly job-specific. Also, performance standards will eventually be written reflecting the content of each work behavior. If there are too many very specific behaviors defining a competency, it becomes difficult to write performance standards that are straightforward and efficient for managers to use. Having performance standards that are clear, uncomplicated, and easy to use is essential for gaining buy-in from users of the system. As a practical matter, it is much more important to cover the essential job content efficiently and effectively than to have highly detailed, cumbersome, and complicated standards. Three sample work behaviors for the Planning Work competency are shown in the example.

Example:
Planning Work Competency and Related Work Behaviors

Planning Work – develops plans and coordinates to complete work according to deadlines and schedules; deals with changing circumstances and makes adjustments to plans to avoid delays.

- Plans, prioritizes, and balances projects and/or assignments to accomplish work in a timely manner.
- Coordinates work with others and keeps them informed of progress and problems.
- Adjusts plans, goals, and priorities to address problems, roadblocks, or changing situations.

Once draft competencies and work behaviors are identified, job experts (i.e., incumbents or supervisors) review and provide feedback on these in a focus group meeting. Job experts are asked to address the following questions:

- Are the competencies comprehensive and correct for the job(s) in question?
- Are the work behaviors defining each competency complete and correct for the job(s) in question?
- What wording changes are revisions are needed to the competency definitions or work behaviors to make them maximally relevant for the job(s)?

Collectively, the job experts attending the focus group meeting should have sufficient knowledge of all of the occupations under consideration so that they can comment on the relevance of the competencies and work behaviors and revise them, if necessary. Participants should be selected to be representative in terms of occupation, location, race, gender, age (over 40), and any other factors that may yield differences in perceptions about the job requirements. Six to 10 participants are typically included in each focus group.

The number of focus groups needed depends on the size of the job incumbent pool and the number of factors that need to be represented (e.g., race, gender, different locations, shifts, etc.). For many jobs, two workshops with a total of 12–15 participants are sufficient to review draft competency and work behavior lists. Obviously, if competencies and work behaviors are being developed to apply across jobs, workshops need to be conducted with job experts who can collectively speak to all of the jobs. The end product of Step 1 is a set of competencies, each defined by approximately five to eight work behaviors that have been reviewed and edited by job experts.

Step 2: Validate Competency Model

To validate the competencies and work behaviors, a survey of job experts is recommended where they are asked to rate the importance of the work behaviors for performing their jobs. Usually, job incumbents are surveyed, although supervisors of the target jobs can also participate in addition to or instead of job incumbents. For validation purposes, it is sufficient to draw a representative sample of respondents to complete the survey. However, to promote buy-in from the workforce, a better strategy is to allow any organizational member who will be covered by the system to complete a survey. This is especially important when a new system is threatening to employees or will involve something new, such as pay tied to performance when this has not been the case in the past. Drawing a sample of respondents is referred to as a sample-based survey. Allowing all affected organizational members to participate is called a census survey.

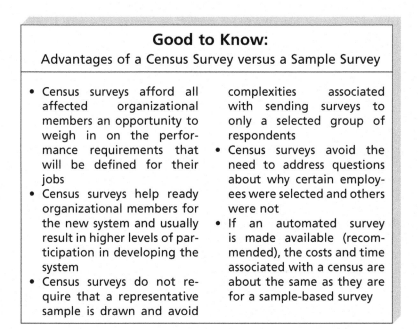

Good to Know:
Advantages of a Census Survey versus a Sample Survey

- Census surveys afford all affected organizational members an opportunity to weigh in on the performance requirements that will be defined for their jobs
- Census surveys help ready organizational members for the new system and usually result in higher levels of participation in developing the system
- Census surveys do not require that a representative sample is drawn and avoid complexities associated with sending surveys to only a selected group of respondents
- Census surveys avoid the need to address questions about why certain employees were selected and others were not
- If an automated survey is made available (recommended), the costs and time associated with a census are about the same as they are for a sample-based survey

The survey data provide a basis for demonstrating that the competencies and work behaviors are job-related, thus addressing both professional and legal standards. The competencies and work behaviors are usually rated on a five-point importance scale, ranging from extremely important (5) to minor importance (1). A response option is also provided for indicating that a work behavior is not relevant to the job. Work behaviors that receive an average rating across respondents of "Important" (3.0) or greater are generally considered to be sufficiently important to be retained. The idea is that it is not appropriate to hold employees accountable for or evaluate their performance on a work behavior that is not an important job requirement. Another criterion that is sometimes used in conjunction with the average importance rating is that not more than 25% of respondents report that a work behavior is Not Relevant for their jobs. In the example below, only the work behaviors are rated for importance and not the competency overall. This is because the competency is defined by the work behaviors. However, if desired, an importance rating of the competency itself can also be collected in the job analysis survey.

Example:
Job Analysis Survey

Welcome

The purpose of this very important survey is to gather information that will be used to develop our new performance management system. Your participation in this effort is vital. It will ensure that the competencies contained in our new performance management system are based on work behaviors that are important and relevant to your job. Therefore, we are asking you to rate the importance of the work behaviors defining each competency.

Rating the Importance of the Work Behaviors

There are eight competencies within this survey. Each competency is defined by a set of work behaviors that you will rate in terms of their importance to *the work you personally perform*. For each behavior, first decide if it is important for effective performance on your job.

- If the behavior is *not* important for effective performance in your work, *click* on the button labeled "NR" for not relevant and move to the next item.
- If the behavior is important for effective performance in your job, *click* on the button that indicates its level of importance using the following scale.

1 = *Minor Importance* for effective performance of my job
2 = *Some Importance* for effective performance of my job
3 = *Important* for effective performance of my job
4 = *Very Important* for effective performance of my job
5 = *Extremely Important* for effective performance of my job

Below is an example of how one person responded to a portion of the survey.

Use the scale on the right to indicate how important each of the work behaviors listed below is for effective performance in your job. To indicate your answer *click* on one of the buttons below.

Importance
NR = Not Relevant to Work
1 = Minor Importance
2 = Some Importance
3 = Important
4 = Very Important
5 = Extremely Important

	NR	1	2	3	4	5
1. Plans, prioritizes, and balances projects and/or assignments to accomplish work in a timely manner.	◉	○	○	○	○	○

	NR	1	2	3	4	5
2. Coordinates work with others and keeps them informed of progress and problems.	○	○	○	○	◉	○

Question 1: The respondent clicked on "NR" to indicate that *"Plans, prioritizes, and balances projects and/or assignments to accomplish work in a timely manner"* is "Not Relevant" to the respondent's work.

Question 2: The respondent clicked on "4" to indicate that *"Coordinates work with others and keeps them informed of progress and problems"* is "Very Important" for effective performance of the respondent's work.

In situations where the competencies and work behaviors will be applied across jobs, it is important to analyze the data separately for the respondents within each job. Likewise, if standards will be written for different experience levels, it is also important to analyze the data separately for respondents who have these different levels of experience. This ensures that the competencies and work behaviors on which the performance standards will be based reflect requirements that are important for each job and level of experience within that job. Sometimes, for example, a work behavior may only be important for employees with higher levels of experience but not at the entry level. Or, a work behavior may apply to only supervisors and managers but not non-supervisory employees. Likewise, although the work behaviors were designed to apply across jobs, some may not be important for certain jobs. If the work behaviors and competencies cannot be shown to be relevant and sufficiently important for each job and each experience level within a job, then slightly different competency models and performance standards will need to be selectively used based on the survey results. Under these circumstances, it may be necessary to remove an entire competency or perhaps one or two work behaviors defining a competency for some jobs or experience levels within those jobs.

An example will help to clarify how the survey data are used. Shown in the example are partial job analysis results for full performance employees in six different jobs. For a work behavior to be retained, we will use two criteria:

- The behavior must have an average importance rating of at least 3.0 ("Important")
- No more than 25% of respondents can report that the behavior is "Not Relevant" for their job

Using these criteria to interpret the data in the example below:

- One behavior is not valid for Support Jobs, *Plans, prioritizes, and balances projects and/or assignments to accomplish work in a timely manner*. This behavior will need to be excluded from the competency model and performance standards for this job.
- Because all three behaviors are not valid for Maintenance Jobs, the entire Planning Work competency will need to be excluded for these jobs.

Example:
Job Analysis Results: Average Importance Rating and % Not Relevant for Full Performance Level Employees in Six Jobs

	Product Development Jobs	Human Resources Jobs	Finance & Accounting Jobs	Support Jobs	Maintenance Jobs	Sales Jobs
Plans, prioritizes, and Balances projects and/or assignments to accomplish work in a timely manner.	4.57 0%	4.36 0%	3.97 0%	2.55 14%	2.55 30%	4.84 0%
Coordinates work with others and keeps them informed of progress and problems.	4.28 5%	4.88 0%	4.5 3%	3.68 14%	2.13 40%	3.76 0%
Adjusts plans, goals, and priorities to address problems, roadblocks, or changing situations.	4.89 0%	4.73 0%	4.69 0%	4.88 0%	2.68 20%	3.69 0%

Step 3: Develop and Confirm Appropriateness of Performance Standards

The development of standards to guide the performance ratings is an important component of a transparent, effective, and fair performance management system. Performance standards need to be written that describe how important work behaviors are performed at different levels of effectiveness. For each work behavior, a standard is written describing the type of performance that would be considered meeting expectations, while a higher-level standard would be written describing the type of performance that would be considered exceeding expectations. Performance standards should be written to be decidedly results-oriented, thus reinforcing the importance of achieving important work outcomes. To incorporate a results focus, the performance standards should not simply describe desirable behaviors, but they should also describe the expected outcomes from these behaviors.

Case Scenario:
Results-Oriented Performance Standards

At a technology development organization, the decision was made to develop results-oriented performance standards, whereby each work behavior would be defined in terms of the results expected from performing that behavior.

One of the work behaviors defining the "Collaboration with Others" competency was:

- "Develop positive, professional, and constructive relationships with team members."

The results-oriented performance standard that was written for this behavior was:

- "Develop positive, professional, and constructive relationships with team members that promote cooperation and collaboration, resulting in efficient completion of team projects, reduced costs of performing work, and completion of work well before due dates."

Typically, initial performance standards are written by Human Resources professionals. To refine the standards, workshops are conducted with representative job experts, who review and comment on the standards and suggest additions, deletions, or revisions. Identification of participants for these workshops needs to follow the same guidelines for representation discussed previously for reviewing the draft competencies and work behaviors.

To validate the standards, another set of workshops is held with job experts who did not participate in the first set of workshops. Participants in these workshops are asked to make ratings regarding whether or not the standards comprehensively measure the important work behaviors. Although the standards were specifically written to reflect different levels of effectiveness in performing the work behaviors, it is possible that some aspects of the work behaviors may have been lost in developing the standards. Accordingly, these ratings help to ensure that the integrity of the work behaviors was retained, supporting the job-relevance of the performance standards and their use as a basis for making human resources decisions.

Workshop participants are also asked to rate the extent to which they feel that the standards accurately describe "Meets" and "Exceeds" performance expectations for the job and experience levels (entry, full-performance, and manager). Since this group of job experts is specifically asked to judge whether the standards appropriately reflect the job requirements for different experience levels, supervisors are usually used because they have knowledge about how the performance expectations change at different job levels.

Example:
Exercise to Finalize Performance Standards

- **Finalizing Competency-based Performance Standards**
The purpose of this task is to ensure that the **performance standards** cover the critical work behaviors and are written to correctly reflect the expectations at different experience and effectiveness levels. You will need to refer to a copy of the performance standards to complete the following two rating tasks.

Continued

- **Task 1: Link the Work Behaviors to the Performance Standards**
  - Read each work behavior and decide which competency's performance standards (titles are across the top) best cover that behavior. Place an "X" in the cell that corresponds to the competency that you feel *best* covers the work behavior.
  - If you encounter a work behavior that you do not feel is covered by any of the performance standards, place an "X" in the column labeled "Work Behavior Not Covered."

Work Behavior	Performance Standards for:			
	Planning Work	Collaboration with Others	Communicating with Others	Work Behavior Not Covered
Plans, prioritizes, and balances projects and/or assignments to accomplish work in a timely manner.				
Adjusts plans, goals, actions, and/or priorities to address problems, roadblocks, or changing situations.				
Adjusts plans, goals, and priorities to address problems, roadblocks, or changing situations.				

- **Task 2: Rate Appropriateness of Expectations for Experience and Effectiveness Levels**
  - Circle "Yes" or "No" to indicate whether you feel the performance standards for each competency properly describe the expectations at the different experience and effectiveness levels.

	Planning Work	Collaboration with Others	Communicating with Others
Do the standards appropriately reflect the performance expected at the different experience levels?	Yes No	Yes No	Yes No
Do the standards appropriately distinguish between *Meets Expectations* and *Exceeds Expectations*?	Yes No	Yes No	Yes No

Different people use different criteria for how much agreement is needed among respondents on the preceding exercise to feel comfortable with the performance standards, ranging from a minimum of 60% to a maximum of 90%. A reasonable level of agreement is 70%. That is, at least 70% of respondents should independently agree that each work behavior is covered by its intended performance standards. At least 70% of respondents should also agree that the standards accurately describe the performance expectations at the different effectiveness and experience levels.

- If less than 70% agree that a behavior is covered by its target competency, this indicates that there is probably redundancy or overlap between the standards for different competencies that might be better differentiated.
- If less than 70% agree that the standards properly describe the expected performance for the different experience and effectiveness levels, this should be further investigated to understand which standards are problematic and revisions should be made accordingly.

Weighting Competencies

Managers and employees frequently jump to the conclusion that competencies should be weighted in deriving an overall rating score. The rationale is that they feel different competencies are more important to overall job success than others. For example, technically-oriented competencies are viewed by some managers as more critical than softer skill competencies, like teamwork and communication. The job analysis data can be used to examine whether there are significant differences in the importance of different competencies and thus if there is any justification for weighting them differently. In most cases, the importance ratings of the competencies that are critical for a job tend to be similar and do not provide support for differential weighting.

Some managers want to go even further than weighting the competencies differently overall. They want to separately weight the competencies for each individual employee to reflect what is most important for that employee's specific work. For development purposes, there is no problem if managers discuss competencies they feel are more or less important for a given employee. However, if performance ratings will be used for decision-making, managers should not idiosyncratically weight competencies for each employee, as this would be akin to holding employees to different standards without justification for doing so.

Contrary to what many intuitively think, the most compelling reason not to differentially weight competencies is that ratings based on weighted and unweighted competencies usually result in the same rank order of employees. If the ratings were used as a basis for decision-making, what this means is that the same decisions would be made about whom to pay more or promote irrespective of whether or not the competencies were differentially weighted. However, so strong is the belief that weighting competencies will make a difference that it is often necessary to perform demonstration studies with real ratings to show that weighted and unweighted competency ratings yield the same rank order of employees.

As a practical matter, since managers sometimes feel strongly that competencies should be weighted and this, in fact, makes virtually no difference in the rank order of employees, one might ask – why not weight the competencies rather than argue the point? The answer is that weighting competencies can add significant administrative burden and cost to a performance management system with no added value. The additional work results from the fact that different weighting algorithms for different jobs (if not individuals) need to be separately and accurately applied when overall rating scores are calculated. The bottom line is that the most effective and efficient choice to make regarding differential weighting of competencies is not to.

Good to Know:
When Is It a Good Idea to Weight Competencies?

Never . . . contrary to what most people think, applying different weights to competencies or performance rating factors results in the same rank order of employees as occurs when no weights are applied. Weighting only serves to increase administrative complexity without producing any differences in end results.

The Bottom Line

Unlike the challenges associated with developing individual objectives, there are virtually no downsides to developing and using performance standards, especially if done in a manner that meets professional standards for validation. Since the process described here provides predefined performance standards that apply across employees, there is no need for managers and employees to devote time or effort to developing standards for each employee's job. The performance standards are easy for managers to use and helpful to employees in understanding their performance requirements. Finally, if written to communicate not only desirable behaviors but the expected results of these behaviors, performance standards also drive employees to focus on achieving important results that contribute to higher-level goals.

Chapter 9

Conclusion

Throughout this book, the focus has been providing practical advice for implementing performance management best practices – and specifically on what it *really takes* to implement these effectively. The goal was to help readers make informed design and implementation decisions, resulting in performance management processes that are a good fit for the organization and work well. To briefly summarize, there are six key take-away points:

- The performance management system must be designed to be congruent with the organization's specific performance management goals.
- Any performance management system needs to be aligned with and support the organization's direction, goals, and critical success factors.
- Successful performance management can be instrumental in driving important outcomes and results, if it is taken advantage of and used properly.
- The culture for performance management in the organization and the appetite of leaders, managers, and staff to engage in performance management activities must be taken into account when making decisions about the complexity of the system, time it requires, and demands it makes. A Volkswagen that helps you get around provides more value than a Mercedes that is never driven.

- Well-developed, efficient tools and processes are essential to make performance management systems user-friendly and well-received.
- You get out of performance management what you put in. The best-developed tools and processes make no difference if users do not believe in the value of performance management and use it as the most important tool they have available to help them get work done.

Notes

2 How Did We Arrive at Today's Best Practices?

1 Muchinsky, P. M. (1997). *Psychology applied to work: An introduction to industrial and organizational psychology.* Pacific Grove, CA: Brooks/Cole Publishing Company.

2 Industrial and Organizational Psychology. Pacific Grove, CA: Brooks/Cole Publishing Company.

3 Patterson, D. G. (1922). The Scott Company graphic rating scale. *Journal of Personnel Research, 1,* 361–376.

4 Austin, J. T., & Villanova, P. (1992). The criterion problem: 1917–1992. *Journal of Applied Psychology, 77,* 836–874.

5 Dunnette, M. D. (1963). A note on the criterion. *Journal of Applied Psychology, 47,* 251–254.

6 Guion, R. M. (1961). Criterion measurement and personnel judgments. *Personnel Psychology, 4,* 141–149.

7 Flanagan, J. C. (1954). The critical incident technique. *Psychological Bulletin, 51,* 327–358; Drucker, P. (1954) *The practice of management.* New York: Harper Row.

8 Smith, P. C., & Kendall, L. M. (1963). Retranslation of expectations: An approach to the construction of unambiguous anchors for rating scales. *Journal of Applied Psychology, 47,* 149–155.

9 Borman, W. C. (1979). Format and training effects on rating accuracy and rating errors. *Journal of Applied Psychology, 64,* 410–421.

10 Borman, W. C., Hough, L. M., & Dunnette, M. D. (1976). *Development of behaviorally based rating scales for evaluating U. S. Navy Recruiters.* (Technical Report TR-76–31). San Diego, CA: Navy Personnel Research and Development Center.

11 Latham, G. P., & Wexley, K. N. (1981). *Increasing productivity through performance appraisal.* Reading, MA: Addison-Wesley.
12 EOCC (1978). Uniform guidelines on employee selection procedures. *Federal register, 43,* 38295–38315.
13 Society for Industrial and Organizational Psychology. (2003). *Principles for the validation and use of personnel selection procedures,* fourth edition. Bowling Green, OH: author.
14 Williams, S. B., & Leavitt, H. J. (1947). Group opinion as a predictor of military leadership. *Journal of Consulting Psychology, 11,* 283–291.
15 Lawler, E. E. (1967). The multitrait-multirater approach to measuring managerial job performance. *Journal of Applied Psychology, 51,* 369–381.
16 Hedge, J. W., Borman, W. C., & Birkeland, S. A. (2001). History and development of multisource feedback as a methodology. In D. W. Bracken, C. W. Timmreck, & Church (Eds.), *The handbook of multisource feedback* (pp. 15–32). San Francisco: Jossey-Bass.
17 Spencer, L., & Spencer, S. (1994). *Competence at work.* New York: John Wiley & Sons, Inc.
18 Pulakos, E. D., Hanson, R. M., & O'Leary, R. D. (2008). Performance management in the United States. In A. Varma, P. Budhwan and A. Denisi (Eds.), *Global performance management.* London: Routledge.
19 Hillgren, J. S., & Cheatham, D. W. (2000). *Understanding performance measures: An approach to linking rewards to the achievement of organizational objectives.* Scottsdale, AZ: World at Work.

3   Getting Started

1 Rotchford, N. L. (2002) Performance management. In J. W. Hedge & E. D. Pulakos (Eds.), *Implementing organizational interventions* (pp. 167–197). San Francisco: Jossey-Bass.
2 Ibid.
3 Greguras, G. J., Robie, C., Schleicher, D. J., Goff, M. (2003). A field study of the effects of rating purpose on the quality of multisource ratings. *Personnel Psychology, 56,* 1–21.
4 Ghorpade, J. (2000). Managing the five paradoxes of 360-degree feedback. *Academy of Management Executive, 14*(1), 140–150.
5 Waldman, D., & Atwater, L. E. (1998). *The power of 360-degree feedback: How to leverage performance evaluations for top productivity.* Houston, TX: Gulf Publishing.
6 Greguras, G. J., Robie, C., Schleicher, D. J., Goff, M. (2003). A field study of the effects of rating purpose on the quality of multisource ratings. *Personnel Psychology, 56,* 1–21.

7 Borman, W. C. (1987). Behavior-based rating scales. In R. A. Berk (Ed.). *Performance assessment: Methods and application*. Baltimore, MD: Johns Hopkins University Press.

8 Rodgers, R., Hunter, J. E., & Rogers, D. L. (1993). Influence of top management commitment on management program success. *Journal of Applied Psychology, 78*, 51–55.

9 Borman, W. C. (1991). Job behavior, performance, and effectiveness. In M. D. Dunnette & L. M. Hough (eds.), *Handbook of industrial and organizational psychology* (vol. 2) (pp. 271–326). Palo Alto, CA: Consulting Psychologists Press.

10 Rodgers, R., Hunter, J. E., & Rogers, D. L. (1993). Influence of top management commitment on management program success. *Journal of Applied Psychology, 78*, 51–55.

11 Engelmann, C. H., & Roesch, R. C. (2001). *Managing individual performance: An approach to designing and effective performance management system*. Scottsdale, AZ: World at Work.

12 Mohrman, A. M., Jr., Resnick-West, S. M., Lawler, E. E. III (1989). *Designing performance appraisal systems: Aligning appraisals and organizational realities*. San Francisco: Jossey-Bass.

4   A Model Performance Management Process

1 Hillgren, J. S., & Cheatham, D. W. (2000). *Understanding performance measures: An approach to linking rewards to the achievement of organizational objectives*. Scottsdale, AZ: World at Work.

2 Ibid.

3 Wexley, K. N. (1986). Appraisal interview. In R. A. Berk (ed.), *Performance assessment*. (pp. 167–185). Baltimore, MD: Johns Hopkins University Press.

4 Ibid.

5 Cederblom, D. (1982). The performance appraisal interview: A review, implications, and suggestions. *Academy of Management Review, 7*, 219–227.

6 Cawley, B. D., Keeping, L. M., & Levy, P. E. (1998). Participation in the performance appraisal process and employee reactions: A meta-analytic review of field investigations. *Journal of Applied Psychology, 83*, 615–633.

7 Wexley, K. N. (1986). Appraisal interview. In R. A. Berk (ed.), *Performance assessment*. (pp. 167–185). Baltimore, MD: Johns Hopkins University Press.

8 Cederblom, D. (1982). The performance appraisal interview: A review, implications, and suggestions. *Academy of Management Review, 7*, 219–227.

9 Hough, L. M., Keyes, M. A., & Dunnette, M. D. (1983). An evaluation of three "alternative" selection procedures. *Personnel Psychology, 36*, 261–276.

10 Gilliland, S. W., & Langdon, J. C. (1998). Creating performance management systems that promote perceptions of fairness. In James W. Smither (ed.)

Performance appraisal: State of the art in practice. San Francisco: Jossey-Bass.

11 Borman, W. C. (1991). Job behavior, performance, and effectiveness. In M. D. Dunnette & L. M. Hough (eds.), *Handbook of industrial and organizational psychology* (vol. 2) (pp. 271–326). Palo Alto, CA: Consulting Psychologists Press.

12 Wexley, K. N. (1986). Appraisal interview. In R. A. Berk (ed.), *Performance assessment.* (pp. 167–185). Baltimore, MD: Johns Hopkins University Press.

5 Performance Management System Implementation

1 Dorsey, D. W. (2002). Information technology. In J. W. Hedge & E. D. Pulakos (Eds.), *Implementing organizational interventions* (pp. 110–132). San Francisco: Jossey-Bass.

2 Summers, L. (2001). Web technologies for administering multisource feedback programs. In D. W. Bracken, C. W. Timmreck, & A. H. Church (Eds.), *The handbook of multisource feedback* (pp. 165–180). San Francisco: Jossey-Bass.

3 Pulakos, E. D. (2004). *Performance management: A roadmap for developing, implementing, and evaluating performance management systems.* Alexandria, VA: Society for Human Resources Management.

6 Legal Requirements

1 Malos, S. (2005). The importance of valid selection and performance appraisal: Do management practices figure in case law? In F. J. Landy (Ed.), *Employment discrimination litigation* (pp. 373–409). San Francisco: Jossey-Bass.

2 EOCC (1978). Uniform guidelines on employee selection procedures. *Federal register, 43,* 38295–38315.

3 Cohen, J. (1988). *Statistical power analysis for the behavioral sciences* (2nd edition). Hillsdale, NJ: Lawrence Erlbaum Associates.

7 Developing Objectives and Measuring Results

1 Locke, E. A., & Latham, G. P. (1990). *A theory of goal setting and task performance.* Englewood Cliffs, NJ: Prentice-Hall.

2 Borman, W. C. (1991). Job behavior, performance, and effectiveness. In M. D. Dunnette & L. M. Hough (eds.), *Handbook of industrial and organizational psychology* (vol. 2) (pp. 271–326). Palo Alto, CA: Consulting Psychologists Press.

3 Jamieson, B. D. (1973). Behavioral problems with management by objective. *Academy of Management Review, 16,* 496–505.
4 Strauss, G. (1972). Management by objectives: A critical review. *Training and Development Journal, 26,* 10–15.
5 Muczyk, J. P. (1979). Dynamics and hazards of MBO application. *Personnel Administrator, 24,* 51–61.
6 Cascio, W. F. (1998). *Applied psychology in human resource management.* Upper Saddle River, NJ: Prentice Hall.
7 Levinson, H. (2005). Management by whose objectives? In *Harvard Business Review on appraising employee performance.* Boston, MA: Harvard Business School Publishing Corporation.

8   Developing Behavioral Performance Standards

1 Spencer, L., & Spencer, S. (1994). *Competence at work.* New York: John Wiley & Sons Inc.
2 Mumford, M. D., & Peterson, N. B. (1999). The O*NET content model: Structural considerations in describing jobs. In N. B. Peterson, M. D. Mumford, W. C. Borman, P. R. Jeanneret, & E. A. Fleishman (Eds.), *An occupational information system for the 21st century: The development of O*NET* (pp. 21–30). Washington, DC: American Psychological Association.
3 Schippmann, J. S. (1999). *Strategic job modeling: Working at the core of integrated human resource systems.* Mahwah, NJ: Lawrence Erlbaum Associates, Inc.

Author Index

Note: Authors not mentioned in the text have a note "n" number after the page reference. More details will be found on pages 185–9.

Subject Index

CPSIA information can be obtained
at www.ICGtesting.com
Printed in the USA
LVOW04s1040050117
519857LV00019B/235/P